D0788548

LONESOME

LONESOME

MEMOIRS OF A
WILDERNESS DOG

Chris Czajkowski
Illustrations by Christina Clarke

TouchWood
Editions

Copyright © 2014 Chris Czajkowski

All rights reserved. No part of this publication may be reproduced, stored in a retrieval system, or transmitted in any form or by any means—electronic, mechanical, recording, or otherwise—without the prior written consent of the publisher or a licence from the Canadian Copyright Licensing Agency (ACCESS Copyright). For a copyright licence, visit accesscopyright.ca.

TouchWood Editions
touchwoodeditions.com

LIBRARY AND ARCHIVES CANADA CATALOGUING IN PUBLICATION
Czajkowski, Chris, author
Lonesome : memoirs of a wilderness dog / Chris Czajkowski. — 10th anniversary edition.

Reprint. Originally published: Victoria, BC : TouchWood Editions, c2004.
Issued in print and electronic formats.
ISBN 978-1-77151-102-5

1. Dogs—British Columbia—Biography. 2. Czajkowski, Chris. 3. Outdoor life—British Columbia. I. Title.

SF426.2.C93 2014   636.70092'9   C2014-902760-5

Cover images: Chris Czajkowski
Illustrations: Christina Clarke
Design: Pete Kohut

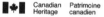

We gratefully acknowledge the financial support for our publishing activities from the Government of Canada through the Canada Book Fund and the Canada Council for the Arts, and from the Province of British Columbia through the British Columbia Arts Council and the Book Publishing Tax Credit.

The interior pages of this book have been printed on 100% post-consumer recycled paper, processed chlorine free, and printed with vegetable-based inks.

1 2 3 4 5 18 17 16 15 14

PRINTED IN CANADA

To
Corry Lunn
and
Uli Augustin
and
everyone who knew
Lonesome,
and to all those who have touched our wilderness.

FOREWORD

LONESOME ISN'T THE ONLY CANINE capable of writing a book, you know. My name is Harry, and I'm about to start writing my own memoirs. (I have to admit that Chris will probably ghost write it; my paws are a bit big to handle a keyboard.)

Chris became part of my life four years ago. Our first meeting was very embarrassing for me: I was wearing a diaper! I bet you didn't know that they even made diapers for dogs. I was rescued off a reserve near Lytton in northern British Columbia and taken to Vancouver. It was there that I had a little adjustment to my anatomy, was put in a crate, and was then flown to a place called Anahim Lake in the Chilcotin. Chris met me at the airport (a battered trailer beside a single runway) and had the sense to take the diaper off at once. There was a snow bank nearby, and I went right over to it and painted it completely yellow. What a relief!

There was another dog in my new pack called Badger, who was a neat old codger. He wasn't very bright, but he was up for adventure and he was a great storyteller. From him, I learned that, in between Lonesome and me, a number of dogs have been part of Chris's pack. They've all had some pretty spectacular adventures. And unless these tales are written down soon, they will be lost, so I reckon this is my mission in life—to record these important pieces of history before it is too late.

Dogs, after all, are natural writers. Chris has written eleven books about her wilderness life, but which is the bestseller? *Lonesome*, of course—the only story told by a dog. Sales of Lonesome's memoir have far surpassed those of any of Chris's other books—and after it was rejected by three publishers who couldn't imagine why people would want to read a book written by a dog. Which just shows how wrong they were. I know my book is going to sell just as well; in fact, I wouldn't be surprised if it surpasses *Lonesome*. After all, I am a superior kind of guy.

Here's an example of how popular *Lonesome* is: Chris has a blog. (That's short for Beautiful, Lovable dOG. Did you know that?) It's a thing she puts on the Internet so that she can tell stories about her life in the bush. On the one hand, Chris loves showing off; on the other, blogging is a more socially acceptable activity among humans than talking to yourself.

Anyhow, because of this blog, a woman from the United States wrote to Chris and started an email discussion about compost toilets (of all things!). After a while, the lady told Chris she was a teacher. At some time in the past, her class had read a book and then had spoken with the author via Skype. Would Chris be interested in doing likewise?

As I said, Chris can never resist a chance to show off, so the school bought enough copies of *Lonesome* for the whole class, and not only did the kids study the book, they also got their pets or favourite animals to "write" *their* own books. The teacher thought it was great, the kids enjoyed the whole process, and Chris basked in all the attention. The teacher is even organizing a similar event for this year.

Be sure to check out that blog (wildernessdweller.ca) if you want to see pictures of me and find out more about Chris's current wilderness home and all of her books (and mine).

In the meantime:

Bark like nobody's listening,
Run like you're beating the wind,
Dig like nobody's watching,
And cherish the bones that you find.

Chow,
Harry

Lonesome is an animal of ancestors nefarious
Her lineage is built upon a pedigree quite various
In fact her canine forefathers were just a mite gregarious
(Although I wouldn't like to say her mother was a slut).
I must, if this verbosity
Has roused your curiosity,
Confess that this monstrosity
Is nothing
But
A mutt.

PROLOGUE

IT WAS NEVER in my nature to seek adventure. Given a choice, I might well have led a life bordering on the mundane and had nothing to write about at all. But fate decreed that I be linked to a human who thrived on what I can only describe as a masochistic delight in physical hardship and deprivation. Short of rebelling against the very principles of my upbringing by disobeying my human outright, I could do nothing but follow along. I feel I have lived up to my ethical code extremely well, despite being sorely tried at times.

You will begin to have an idea as to what I have endured when I tell you that my human, Chris, is a wilderness dweller who lives a day-and-a-half's walk (at human speed) from the nearest road and neighbour, at an altitude of 5,000 feet up in the Canadian mountains. (Sorry about the old-fashioned figures; I'm afraid I never quite caught on to this metric business.) But before she went to that location, she lived in a lower valley, about 40 miles away in British Columbia's Tweedsmuir Provincial Park. That place was also a long way from a road, and reaching it often required an overnight camp. It was where Chris started her wilderness existence, and it was also where I began mine. I was born right in that park a little before Chris came into the country; I have thus been with her during all her formative years in the wild. I have stories of storms and ice and moose and wolves and bears and puppies and tree-planting camps—sometimes I wonder if I might have been a cat in

1

a previous existence, for I certainly went through a number of lives in this one. And the things I could tell you about Chris! But I am not a vindictive creature, and this book will remain fit for family reading throughout.

Chris gave me the idea of describing my adventures in this way because she is herself a published writer. She has detailed her escapades at great length in a number of books and articles. She has, however, been considerably remiss in acknowledging my contributions to her lifestyle during this last decade and a half. Chris's accounts of our adventures are hopelessly biased; they glorify her own accomplishments to the exclusion of my own. True, I have been mentioned once or twice—my most terrifying encounter with a bear was portrayed in *Diary of a Wilderness Dweller*, and in *Cabin at Singing River* I was referred to occasionally—but only as "the dog." And yet, without my unfailing support, it is doubtful that Chris would have got anywhere with her endeavours. This memoir is an attempt to set the record straight.

At the beginning of many books it is customary to see a disclaimer stating that the characters portrayed bear no relationship to anyone living or dead. But this account is, I assure you, all perfectly true. I have simply changed a few names to protect the privacy of the dogs.

Lonesome

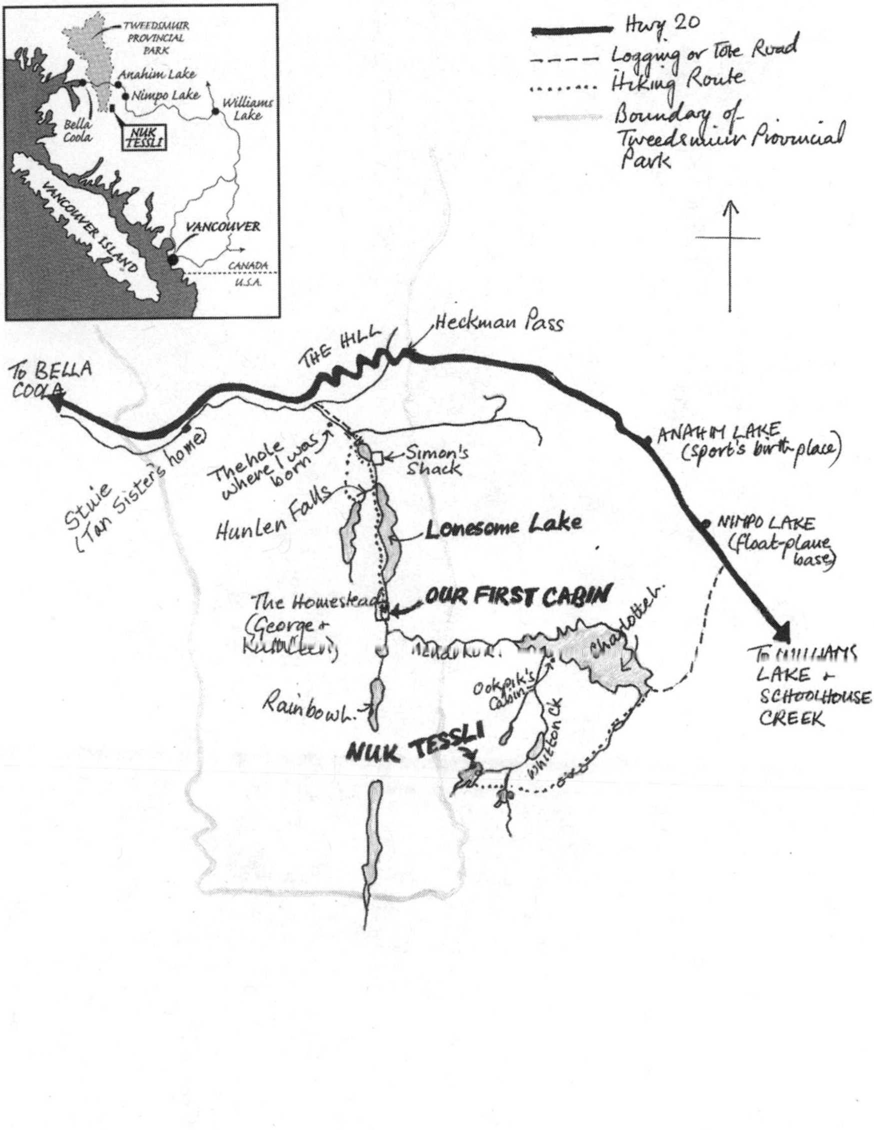

TWEEDSMUIR PROVINCIAL PARK
Anahim Lake
Nimpo Lake
Williams Lake
Bella Coola
NUK TESSLI
VANCOUVER ISLAND
VANCOUVER
CANADA
U.S.A.
Hwy 20
Logging or Tote Road
Hiking Route
Boundary of Tweedsmuir Provincial Park
Heckman Pass
THE HILL
To BELLA COOLA
Stuie (Tan Sister's home)
The hole where I was born
Simon's Shack
Hunlen Falls
Lonesome Lake
ANAHIM LAKE (Sport's birth place)
NIMPO LAKE (float-plane base)
The Homestead (George +
OUR FIRST CABIN
Charlotte L.
Ookpik's Cabin
Whitton Ck
Rainbow L.
NUK TESSLI
LAKE + SCHOOLHOUSE CREEK

None of my brothers and sisters looked much alike—
I was the black shaggy one with three white feet.

CHAPTER ONE

I GOT MY HUMAN WHEN she was already fully grown, which was a relief. I don't like the puppy stage. It's far too unreliable—dangerous, even. You risk your life every time you get in a car with them when they're that age.

But my human was already 33 years old. You have to divide by seven to get the dog equivalent, which made her around five. She should, therefore, have been a well-developed adult, and she certainly was in the physical sense, but whether she was beyond a juvenile level in the mental department remains a moot point. I was clearly paired with an unusual specimen. I'm not a dog to seek adventure and would have been far happier in an orderly, suburban garden with kids to play with and nice, safe walks in the park. I would probably have even had a bed inside a house with that kind of life. But I was the one who had to be landed with an eccentric, someone who flung herself—and me—into the most uncomfortable and unnecessary situations, just because, she said, she liked a challenge.

Challenge indeed! Our lives are brief enough without desiring to end them sooner by leaping off into the great unknown. On my human's account I've forded rivers, swum lakes, ploughed through deep, wet snow well over my head, slept out in the bitterest cold, been tormented by bloodsucking insects and tangled with dangerous animals like porcupines, wolves—and bears. Yes, bears! I shudder to think about them, but they've been common enough in my life, I can tell you. It's a wonder I'm still around to tell this tale.

Ah well, a dog doesn't usually have a lot of choice as to where he or she ends up. And any canine worth her Milk-Bones must take life as it comes and not complain about it.

Among the oddest of my person's abnormal traits is her desire for solitude; all her other peculiarities probably stem from that. It is very untypical of humans to avoid the society of their own species, particularly for females, who are generally less aggressive and easier to control than males. But not this one. She prefers great moose monsters for neighbours rather than a cozy bridge circle, and a gathering of trumpeter swans to an office party. She spends short periods of time with her fellow humans, but after a week or two, off she goes again into that great, unfriendly, useless lump of real estate that many humans rave about, but which most very sensibly avoid. And what else could I do but tag along? Obedience is the code by which I am destined to live; I like to think I have stuck by that code despite great inducement to the contrary.

This solitude business was the hardest of my person's eccentricities to put up with. I'm a gregarious creature myself, probably because I came from a large family whose proud lineage can be traced back for many generations in the area—which is more than could be said for my human. She was very much a newcomer to the district when we met; her nearest relatives lived thousands of miles away, in a different country even. No one knew who they were or anything about them. My pedigree is faithfully recorded, particularly on my mother's side. She was a black Lab (more or less); her mother was a border collie—a pretty fancy-looking bitch she was, too. My great-grandmother was a red terrier, and her maternal ancestor was, so I have been informed, a chihuahua.

All breeds of great integrity, as I am sure you well know. On my father's side my progenitors were no doubt just as noble, but I must confess they are not as well documented. Father was an Old English sheepdog–red setter cross, but my knowledge stops there. I did hear someone mention those dreaded words "dog pound" in connection with my paternal grandfather, but naturally that was all hushed up.

Needless to say, with such a lot of diverse forebears, none of my brothers and sisters looked much alike. There were black smooth-haired ones, smooth yellow-haired ones, fluffy yellow ones, a black shaggy one with three white feet (this was me), and a wiry-haired tan and grey specimen. She had a very pretty face, and she was the first to go.

Not that I understood the nature of her disappearance at the time. I was still very young, not yet properly weaned. The sum total of my world was the comfortable hole in which I was born, the warm bodies with which I shared it, and the beings that inhabited the plywood shack above it. These comprised a multitude of skinny black cats and a very tall human male who bore a long, unkempt beard and was hardly fatter than the felines whose abode he shared. The cats ignored us for the most part, occasionally hissing at us if we inadvertently grabbed a part of their anatomy in our baby teeth, but the old man was very attached to us, often lifting us up and cuddling us in his thin, bony hands. These were completely hairless, and my first memory of them was that they smelled nothing like a dog.

The human would make sounds at us in a dry, cobwebby voice, sounds whose literal meanings meant nothing to me then, but which were inevitably friendly in tone. No doubt my mother was glad to relinquish some degree of our care to the old man, for when she was with us, we did not give her a moment's rest.

Even after Tan Sister left us so abruptly, I had not the slightest intimation that anything would change for me. I thought that life, centred around the spring-warm hole full of tails and ears to chew, would go on forever. Ah, the innocence of puppyhood!

One day, a strange human arrived—strange to me, that is, but she and the old man seemed to be friends, for they greeted each other only briefly, with a smile and a casual exclamation in the way that I now know is normal for humans who are familiar with each other. They talked for a while. The soft roar of the Coleman stove preceded the hiss of the boiling kettle, and soon the two humans were sitting on the step of the shack, holding mugs of a hot, bitter-smelling liquid. My mother had escaped family pressures for a while, and we puppies lay in a sun-warmed, dozing huddle close to the humans' feet. The newcomer's voice was quite irritating, being high-pitched and very loud. (The pitch, I discovered later, was because she was female—the sexes can often be told apart by voice alone—but the loudness, thank goodness, was only temporary; the old man had lost most of his hearing.)

I expect you have guessed what happened. Without any warning, this strange human suddenly rose to her feet, took two steps toward me and scooped me up in her hands. I didn't like that much; her hands smelled nothing like the old man's. I simply lay there and hoped that if I closed my eyes she would put me back and go away. Then she spoke. "I'll take this one," she said. I was not conversant with human language then, but the sounds echo as clearly through the tunnel of years as if I had heard them yesterday, for they were the seal to my fate.

The strange human's hands held me firmly, and then she started to walk. Her heavy-footed, long-striding gait lurched me back and forth, but the fingers clutched me tightly and I could not have fallen free even if I had wanted to. I had no defence against this unpleasant sensation other than to keep my eyes closed, with the hope that things would revert to normal any moment if only I lay inert. But the lurching went on for a long time, and eventually another smell registered among my senses, a smell that I would learn to hate. The old man carried a similar aroma home with him when he had been away for the day, but I had never encountered anything like a motor vehicle before. The human opened the side of this contraption and bent herself onto the seat. The hands released me, and I was now supported by her thighs. That might have been tolerable, but I was totally unprepared for the sudden harsh choking, worse than a dozen ravens with fish bones in their throats, that went on and on and then leapt into a mighty roar louder than the river that ran not far from the old man's shack, which was, at this time, flooded with snowmelt. I writhed in terror, whimpering at the noise and the hideous vibration that accompanied it. "Sorry, little puppy," said the person. "It must be pretty frightening, but you'll have to put up with it for a couple of days. We're a long way from home." She tried to give me comfort with her hands, but these were soon occupied with other activities, and besides, I don't think anything could have consoled me then.

I can look back with the experience of years and know that the first part of the drive was not on a typical road. But at first I thought that the insane tossing and heaving were the normal result of being ensnared in such a behemoth; I had no idea that such torture had any kind of purpose. At the time, it was simply a nightmare. After a while, the violence of the movement lessened and the motor noise rose in pitch; it became not unlike the purring of a very loud cat. I was lulled somewhat by the reduction of movement, but eventually the sound and rhythm changed again, then shortly ceased. What blessed silence!

However, another fright was in store for me. The person picked me up in her hands again and deposited me in a huge, metal-walled enclosure that rested behind the cab we had been sitting in. The enclosure was naked except for an old empty sack in the corner. It smelled somewhat of the human, but overpoweringly of the vehicle. I was to know this box on the back of the pickup well in later years, but then, like everything else, it was simply incomprehensible. I kept to my customary practice of lying still with my eyes closed, but now there was not even the warmth of the human to console me. It finally dawned on me that such passive resistance was not improving my lot. Once, when I was still at home with my brothers and sisters, I had wandered free from the hole and become lost. I at once gave a great, piercing yell, and my mother found me very quickly. Perhaps if I called her now, she would come and fetch me again.

The yipping had an effect, all right, but it was not my mother who came. There was the immediate sound of heavy human feet thumping the ground, and the top portion of the person who had abducted me suddenly loomed against the vast, lonely rectangle of the sky. She was laughing, and she stretched those great arms toward me and picked me up. Another human stood beside her. This one was also female, but shorter and much older. I had no idea there were so many people in the world! I stopped yelling as I did not know what to do next, and the two humans oohed and aahed at me for a while, sounding not unlike the bleating mountain goats who inhabited the rock faces above my home.

"Well, that's one less that Simon has to find a home for," said the older lady. "It really is too bad that he does nothing to prevent his dog from having puppies that no one wants. I hear Debbie and Michael have one; perhaps I should take one off his hands, too. I haven't had a dog for 12 years, but now that Tom's dead, it would be company for me."

"I'd better take a rain check on that cup of tea," said my human, still holding me. "I can't leave the puppy alone or your neighbours will think you're murdering something. What a yell! Who would have thought that such a little scrap could make such a big noise!"

"Look at the funny hairs around her muzzle!" exclaimed the older lady, bringing her face close to mine. (That was the first time I knew there was anything funny about my hairs.) "Looks like she's going to have a wiry muzzle and smoother body." She ran her hands gently over my face and rubbed me between the ears, a rather pleasing sensation not unlike Mother's lick. "Have you got a name for her?"

"I was thinking of calling her Lonesome because of the lake. After her dramatic demonstration just now, I think that might be quite appropriate."

"When will you be back?" the lady asked as she stepped away.

"I'm not sure. I promised to help a neighbour make hay this summer, and I have an art show coming up in the fall—I can sure use the money. Once I bury myself in the woods out there, I won't have a lot of chances to earn cash. All being well, I'll be back here again next spring. She," (the human indicated me with her hands) "will be big enough to walk in and out on her own then; now I'd have to carry her everywhere."

"That's true." A laugh. "Well, Chris, take care. Have a good journey and we'll see you next year."

At which I was deposited inside the stinking cab once more. The ghastly choking-raven noises started again, and for the second time I was subjected to the distress of motor travel. This journey went on for a very long time. There were a large number of boxes and cartons in the cab. I crawled into a little hole between a couple of them—the proximity of the solid surfaces gave me a small feeling of security—and fell into a bewildered trance of misery.

CHAPTER TWO

I HAD BEGUN TO THINK that truck travel was all there was to Life Beyond The Hole. But sometime during the following day we turned off the road onto a grassy track, staggered and jerked through a couple of gates and finally stopped.

"This is it, pup," said my human. She pulled me from where I had been hiding among the boxes, picked me up and put me on the ground. I surveyed my surroundings blearily. The truck was parked close to a little cedar tree, beside which was a wooden shack not much bigger than the one above the hole where I was born. Chris's shack, however, smelled quite different—partly, I was to discover, because there were no cats in it, and partly because, unlike the old man, Chris periodically went through the peculiar process of soaking both her clothes and herself in soapy water. It was something I had never seen the old man do. This action had the effect of changing human odours dramatically.

Around the shack, the grass-covered, gently sloping ground was neatly bisected by a split-rail fence. I was dimly aware of hills and patches of forest at the edges of my vision. The forest scents were familiar, being much like those of home, but there were strange animals scattered about the grass. These, I soon learned, were part of the extended families that some of Chris's neighbours affected. To me, most of these creatures were enormous, dull and stupid, and more than a little frightening, but they were generally easy to avoid.

Apart from that, Chris's shack proved to be a pleasant place;

even in that first encounter, the relief of not having to travel in the truck anymore made me almost cheerful. I hate to admit that the memory of the family from which I had been so recently and cruelly wrenched was already starting to fade, but then, most young things are resilient creatures and have a good degree of built-in optimism. As long as my surrogate mother—my human, that is—was within reach of my ears and nose, life did not seem too bad.

At first, Chris gave me a box inside the shack for a bed, but the place being small and filled with a lot more possessions than the old man ever owned, the box was soon relegated to a lean-to at one end. I was never a bothersome puppy. My mother had impressed upon me the importance of good manners, and I have faithfully followed that creed all my life. I never once disgraced myself in the house, nor did I ever have a serious problem during the chewing stage. My human was much more stern with me than most people are with their dogs (as I later found out), allowing me to deviate from her requirements not a whit. Sometimes I found these dictates extremely puzzling, such as having to *Sit* and *Stay* while my human backed away from me, but my innate obedience won the day, and as soon as I realized what was required of me, my only desire was to please.

Humans are extremely egotistical creatures. They seem to have no idea that there might be other ways than their own of looking at life. However, I had to admit that my human was one of the smarter ones. Sometimes she seemed to understand almost everything I said.

Few humans master interspecies languages with any degree of facility, although most of them pick up a few basic signals of dogspeak, such as a growl of anger, the whine or door scratch when desiring to go in or out, or the pathetic, mute appeal that is so useful for getting a treat. (My human, I should add here, was singularly unresponsive to that expression, and I never employed it when dealing with her. Anyone else, however, was fair game. Now this is an oddity—explain it to me if you can. When a human puts on a begging expression, that person is usually ostracized by his own species, but when a dog employs the same technique, the majority of humans immediately respond with gooey-eyed affection.)

Many canines soon learn to recognize a considerable number of human words, but body language is a far more effective method of communication between the species. Like us, humans have mobile eyebrows and lips; they vary the shape of their mouths and the amount of teeth and gums that they show. The angle of their bodies and droop of their shoulders speak volumes. However, humans seem to put little store by these dialects; I can only assume that this is because they do not possess that most expressive of organs: the tail. They have to compensate by uttering an enormously complicated range of vocal sounds. They rely so completely on this audible vocabulary that they often forget they have any body language at all. This frequently results in their using words to say one thing when they quite obviously mean something entirely different.

In this, my human was typical. When speaking to me she would think it necessary to exaggerate her features into a cartoon expression, apparently not realizing that I could read very small movements of her face. I figured that because she used such excessive body signals, I was obliged to respond to the same degree, and I would produce a wriggling, ear-flattening grin to denote pleasure, or droop my ears and shove my tail between my legs when I wanted to be forgiven for doing something of which she did not approve (even though the reason for her disapproval might have been extremely mystifying, and I actually felt no remorse at all. However, I always considered it politic to go through the motions).

Even Chris, however, sometimes took an awfully long time to pick up on things. I often heard her say to a neighbour that she was puzzled as to how I could tell the difference between her putting on her boots to go to the outhouse and putting on her boots to go for a walk. With the former I barely raised an eyebrow, and with the latter I would leap about excitedly in the manner she seemed to expect of me when we were about to set off for a you-know-what. (Humans so often interchange that phrase with enjoyable happenings that I am never quite sure which is correct.) However, Chris hit on the right solution in the end. It was, of course, the laces. Even when I was outside the closed door, I had no trouble hearing the nylon fabric slide through the metal-rimmed holes in the boots. Tightened laces meant an excursion; no tightening meant nothing to get excited about at all.

Ah, neighbours. We had them in those days. We were partway up a slope, and I could see six other houses scattered around the partly treed valley. The nearest was up the hill behind us. Two people lived there, and their extended family included a dozen sheep and another dog. Chris used to go up there to buy eggs. Not far from the house was a small building about the size of Chris's shack; it was surrounded by a close-meshed wire fence, and in it were a number of dumpy, feathery creatures called chickens. Such flighty and hysterical creatures were beyond my ken; so was the idea of shutting something up in a wire pen. Chris saw me staring intently at them and said at once, "Lonesome, don't you even *think* about it," in such a sharp voice that I realized immediately that chickens are of a class so far beneath us that it is an embarrassment to be seen taking an interest in them. I have treated them with suitable disdain ever since.

*I realized immediately that chickens are of a class so far beneath
us that it is an embarrassment to be seen taking an interest in
them. I have treated them with suitable disdain ever since.*

The dog who lived there was a collie, not unlike my maternal grandmother in appearance, but without her panache. He was a year older than I was, and although he was a somewhat ineffectual being, I enjoyed playing with him so much that it wasn't long before I would run up to his house without waiting for my human to go. For some reason, this displeased Chris mightily. She would come striding up the hill after me and speak very harshly to me. I would always hang my head and look suitably contrite, but it was not long before I was back there again. I couldn't help it; Egg Lady was so friendly. She would say, "Oh, Lonesome! You bad dog." These words, taken at their face value, meant that I had done something wrong. However, she uttered them in such a gentle tone, and she patted me and gave me such a friendly look, that I knew she did not mean it. But one time when my human came after me, I was given a smack. This was the first time Chris had ever chastised me with the severity that my mother used to employ, and it showed me at once that puzzling though this misdemeanour was to me, Chris considered it serious. I never did it again.

I received a wallop from my human on only one other occasion, and it was a really good one. Outside Chris's shack was a low picnic table. Chris often sat out there to work and eat, and one day the table was graced by a chunk of meat. As the table was so low, it was an easy matter for my rapidly growing legs to carry me onto it. At the very moment my jaws were about to close on the meat, my human roared, and I received a swipe of such immensity that I was flung clean off the table and onto the grass. "No! No! No!" Chris yelled. Her eyebrows were yanked together, and her eyes flashed sparks. "Never, never, NEVER do that AGAIN!" She waggled a rigid forefinger at me and parodied furious rage for the next half-hour, even though I could tell that it was only in the first instance that she was really angry. However, I played along and looked steadfastly dejected until she smiled at me again. It was, needless to say, a pretty clear message, and I've never since eaten food of any sort unless I've been told that I can have it.

🍂

I WAS ONLY a few months old when a dog from the nearby town of Salmon Arm came to live with us. Apparently his human was sick, and he needed a temporary home. He was much smaller than I was (I had grown considerably by then; I doubt that my own mother would have recognized me), but Snoopy (for such was the name that his human had given him) was already fully grown. Despite his superior age, he was amazingly stupid. When we went on our first walk, he had no idea how to wriggle through a fence. Chris climbed over; I quickly popped through a convenient hole, but Snoopy, even though he barely had to bend to squeeze under the bottom rail, stood there and whimpered. Chris gave him very short shrift about that; she simply walked on and ignored him. He soon learned to negotiate fences, but it makes one wonder about the kind of education most of these city dogs have. They think themselves superior because they know about things like traffic lights and mail carriers, but put them in an unfamiliar environment and they fall apart very quickly. As more canines now live in cities than in the country and therefore dictate most of the policies of our society, it makes one seriously despair about the future of the world.

Snoopy wasn't a particularly lovable animal, being a whiner outside doors and otherwise having an irascible disposition, but he had one passion that he passed on to me: squeakers.

The country was full of them. They sat upright on mounds of dirt beside their burrows, their little paws neatly folded against their chests. If alarmed, they gave a piercing *peek!* and bolted down their burrows. Chris referred to these creatures as ground squirrels. I felt no personal antagonism toward them, but I soon learned that their whistle was a signal to run. Off I would go in a glorious gallop behind Snoopy's wiry body until we hit the ground squirrel's heap of dirt. The owner of the mound was, of course, long gone by then, and I was never quite sure what to do when we got there, but Snoopy seemed to think he had won a great victory. He would march stiff-legged back to the shack, his ridiculous tail (which can't have had more than six hairs on it) stuck straight up in the air.

One day, Chris did a curious thing. She picked up a stick and tossed it. I stood perfectly still, following it with the motion of my head, and watched it fly through the air and thump to the ground. What was all that about? Snoopy, however, must have had some previous experience with this mysterious manoeuvre, for he immediately tore after the stick. Was this, like the squeakers, another excuse for running? I lollopped over to join the fun, but Snoopy growled and snapped in a most unpleasant manner. Soon the stick was nothing but pulp and splinters. Chris threw another one. I watched it; Snoopy ran; I followed and was again rebuffed in no uncertain manner. I immediately lost interest in this activity, being obviously not welcome and having not the remotest idea as to its benefit. Chris never did it again. It was merely one of many human idiosyncrasies that seemed to make no sense.

Snoopy stayed with us for three months, and on the whole I cannot say I was sorry to see him go.

I LEARNED A lot about farming while we lived in that shack. Chris would often help the neighbours make hay or feed their animals, and she sometimes milked their house cows when they went away. Most of these animals were big and clumsy, and they possessed an intelligence of inverse proportion to their size. The person who owned the land on which we lived sometimes put her cows and sheep into the fields around the shack. At those times, Chris would shut the sheep up in a corral at night. This was for their own good; even though there were so many of them, they did not have the wits to defend themselves against the roving mobs of coyotes that were predominant in that area. Chris's neighbours invariably spoke of these dangerous gangsters with harsh vowels and lips thinned and turned down at the corners. I could not help but agree. These lawless savages made a mockery of all that Man's Best Friend stood for. Chris, however, seemed curiously ambivalent toward them. Would that I had understood where such an attitude was going to lead us, for I might, at that early stage, have been able to do something about it.

"Come on, Lonesome," Chris would say to me when she had to shut up the sheep. "Your grandmother was a collie and your father part English sheepdog. You're supposed to be good at this." She would then wave her arms and make a sort of *ch ch ch ch ch!* noise, running jerkily behind the sheep, dodging first to one side and then to the other. The sheep knew very well where they were supposed to go, but they never cooperated. I was not as much help as I would have liked to be, for I was not sure what I was supposed to do. I could neither wave my arms nor make that strange *ch ch ch ch ch!* noise, which I assumed to be a misguided human attempt at sheepspeak. In any case, those smelly, woolly creatures were all bigger than I was, and every one had an aggressive glint in its hard, yellow eyes.

WHEN I WAS nine months old, I awoke to a curious phenomenon (curious, at least, to my young brain. I have heard since that there are parts of the world where it never occurs; would that my fate had placed me in one of them).

Overnight, the world changed. It looked rather as if someone had taken the white sheets Chris sometimes hung on a line and enlarged them and draped them all over the trees and fences and fields. The texture of this covering was, however, unlike any fabric I had seen. For a start, it was cold—most unpleasantly so. Secondly, it was so fragile, it disintegrated at a touch. My feet left holes in it, the shape of each of my paws perfectly reproduced. It smelled like rain, and I rapidly discovered it was equally wet. I had always hated water and had generally gone to great lengths to keep my feet dry. With this stuff, it was impossible. It was everywhere. Moreover, it kept tumbling from the sky, in particles that looked very like what happened to the toilet paper when Chris left the lid off the coffee can in the outhouse and the mice got into it.

"Well, it may have come late, but we're sure getting enough now that it's started," my human and Egg Lady would say almost every time they met. Every day, more of the stuff would fall, and it soon became alarmingly deep. My human donned long, thin shoes called skis, and every day she would plod up the hill behind the shack, work her way along some of the overgrown logging roads near the edge of the forest, swoop down toward the hay farmer's buildings, then shuffle back along the lower fields to the shack. Deeper and deeper grew the snow; soon Chris sank to her knees at every step, and I could make progress, even in her ski tracks, only with the greatest difficulty. I once discovered that if I kept very close behind her I could stand on the backs of the skis, which helped considerably, but Chris poked me with a ski pole and let me know in no uncertain terms that she was

Even walking in Chris's ski tracks, I could make progress through the deepening snow only with the greatest difficulty.

not going to allow that. It seemed a little unfair, as she herself could not have waded through the snow unaided, and yet she expected me, with my much shorter legs, to cope as best I could. What was worse, the snow seeped into the fur against my belly and made ice balls between my toes. These were very uncomfortable, and I had to stop continually to bite them out. The snow also plastered itself over my face until only my eyes were uncovered. The more I tried to rub my face clean, the more the snow stuck to it.

My human seemed to find this hilarious. She would obscure the front of her head with a device called a camera and transfix me with its great black piercing eye. There would be a click, and her face would appear again, grinning unsympathetically. "You might as well get used to this, Lonesome," she would say. "You're going to see a lot more of it where we're going."

It was an unusually deep-snow winter for that part of the world, I inferred from comments between Chris and Egg Lady, and soon even the fences were covered. However, the snow later thawed and froze, so that at first Chris's skis, and later my feet, barely sank at all. At that stage, Chris seemed to spend most of her downhill time extracting herself from head-first tumbles into drifts, but for me it was a lot better. I could run into the woods and investigate the holes that occurred under fallen trees and around rocks. The holes were often framed by large, feathery frost crystals. The aromas that issued forth from these natural vents were always very interesting.

Finally, the snow began to melt. As the sodden, muddied ground emerged, a zillion pocket-gopher tunnels appeared in the fields. Completely hidden by the snow, these little creatures had built impressive cities of round grass houses with separate adjoining bathrooms linked by long, wriggling thoroughfares. Although many of them were flooded out during the thaw, some were still occupied, and I loved to pounce on the tantalizing rustles as their inhabitants moved swiftly away through the old alfalfa stalks.

And the day the last patch of snow disappeared from the hill behind us, the first ground squirrel emerged from its burrow. Snoopy had left by then, but the squeak was enough to send me streaking in the squirrel's direction. For me, that sound will always mean youth and springtime, and I have never failed to respond to it.

I SHALL BACKTRACK here for a moment, for at the beginning of winter I had an extremely unpleasant experience. I had gradually overcome my terror of (if not my repugnance for) the truck, and I would accompany my human when she went to town. I usually rode in the back; at first I was tied in with a rope (which I hated), but soon Chris had enough faith in me to leave me unfastened. Unfortunately, young animals occasionally misuse the trust placed in them, and one day while my human was in the library, I decided to hop out and have a bit of a walk. I had taken no more than a few steps when a fat little man stopped in front of me.

I would no more forget how to greet a human properly than lose track of my food dish, and almost always I could expect politeness in return. But on this occasion, I hardly had time to wag my tail before the man put a string around my neck and dragged me along the sidewalk. I tried to get back into our truck, which was just across the road, but to no avail. I was bundled into another pickup with a closed back and driven away.

"I came out of the library," said my human to Egg Lady afterward, "and there was no dog. There was a bit of snow on the ground and a few doggy footprints in it, but they were pretty scuffed over. I walked around a bit calling, 'Lonesome! Lonesome!'"

Upon which Egg Lady guffawed. "Oh, Chris!" she said. "You shouldn't wander around saying 'Lonesome, Lonesome.' People might get the wrong idea!"

Chris snorted and giggled (for a reason that escaped me), and it was a moment before she could continue. "I didn't know what to do. She's never jumped out of the truck before. But I needed some gas and drove into that station by the library. I thought I might as well ask the guy if he'd seen anything like Lonesome. He said the dog catcher had just gassed up; he had a huge black shaggy dog in the back. Well, Lonesome isn't all that big, but she's more or less black and definitely shaggy. So I phoned him and sure enough, that's where she was. He's way out of town in a real wrecky house with a sagging porch and a bunch of great steel-meshed pens out the back. Lonesome was the only dog in there. He'd had her there for 20 minutes and charged me 35 bucks, so you can imagine how pleased I was about that."

"You were lucky he didn't make you buy a licence as well," replied Egg Lady. "They do that sometimes, even if you *do* live outside the city limits. I've heard all sorts of stories about this dog catcher. He only impounds friendly dogs. If they're at all vicious, he'll do anything to get out of handling them."

"That's Lonesome's trouble. She's just too friendly. I guess it's impossible to teach a dog not to speak to strangers. Still, I'd rather have her that way than be forever restraining her when anyone comes." At which point in the story (for it was repeated to all the neighbours in turn), I would know a pat was forthcoming—whether from my human or the other person, it didn't matter—and position myself accordingly. "Look at her," my human would say, as my ears were deliciously tickled. "She knows we're talking about her." As if I could possibly mistake it!

Needless to say, for all the attention it gave me, the shame of the experience was with me for a long time. Firstly, I was conscious of the indignity of being treated no better than a chicken, and secondly, I was reminded of my paternal grandfather's association with the dog pound and the very real disgrace that was attached to it.

✿

LIKE ALL YOUNG things, I had little thought of the future and had long forgotten much of my infancy. I had, therefore, no inkling that my life was going to change. But one day soon after winter had ended and the world was starting to look green and good again, my human began to behave oddly. She started to go through everything in the cabin, burning papers and shoving all her odds and ends into cartons she had picked up on her last trip to town. She was extremely bad-tempered and often snapped at me for no reason that I could see. Wanting to give her some support, I stayed pretty close to her heels at first, but that seemed to make her madder than ever. So I parked myself by the door and lay on my stomach with my head on my paws, keeping my eyes fixed unblinkingly on her face.

Chris's truck did not have a cap or camper like those of many of her friends; the box (as I knew, to my cost) was wide open to the sky. Chris built a wooden rack around it to make the walls higher and started tossing in the boxes of possessions. These included a lot of things I was as yet unfamiliar with, tools mostly, that she had recently acquired from a young man across town. This fellow was apparently desirous of getting married; his only problem was that his intended was in Fiji (where, I learned, there lived a different breed of human altogether). The young man was

*Chris's truck loaded up with boxes—the first of
many relocations we'd complete over the years.*

selling everything he could to pay for his fare. One of the objects that thus changed hands was very large and very peculiar. Partly because of its hue, and partly because of its shape, it reminded me of the pea pods that Chris discarded into the compost heap after extracting their strange, round meats, which she showed every evidence of enjoying, but which I found remarkably tasteless. This pea-pod-like object, which Chris called a canoe, was enormous and made of a very rigid substance. It was extremely heavy, and because the only place to carry it was right on top of the load, it created more ill humour to get it up there than all the rest of these inexplicable activities put together. Humans are never slow to use their vocal sounds in times of stress, and I was able to extend my knowledge of human vocabulary quite significantly during this operation.

Even the cab of the truck was stuffed full of boxes, and when a bag of dog food and my dish were loaded aboard, I became seriously alarmed. Presumably we were going somewhere, but there did not seem to be any place left for me. I was no longer the little fuzzy ball of puppy fat I had been when I had first arrived; the gaps I had crawled into then were now hopelessly inadequate. However, Chris opened the passenger door of the cab and encouraged me to jump in. I stood there, bewildered, as I could see nothing but a wall of boxes; nonetheless, with Chris boosting me up, I managed to scramble on top of them. Between the top of the boxes and the roof there was just enough room for me. It was a rather unusual place from which to survey the world, but not an uninteresting one.

Chris slammed my door and climbed in the other side. The choking-raven sound, with which I was by now extremely familiar, presaged the lurching of the vehicle down the grassy track, through the gates and onto the road. The wooden crate protested creakily, and the canoe's front end, which jutted like the bill of a cap over the front of the cab, swayed jerkily from side to side. As we moved round onto the highway, I could look back across the field toward the little shack. Its windows reflected the dull sky blankly, and it looked suddenly forlorn and lonely beneath its cedar tree.

Knowing what I do now, with years of unlooked-for adventures behind me, I can never witness any form of packing without a distinct feeling of foreboding.

CHAPTER THREE

DURING THE WHOLE OF THAT first day, we travelled on a busy highway. For a while I found the wherewithal to raise a disapproving eyebrow at dogs in other cars who were either sufficiently ill-mannered to pull faces or simply uncaring enough of their dignity to thrust their noses out of the window and allow their ears to flop and flutter like deflated balloons. Barking dogs were, needless to say, ignored. But what with the unaccustomed heat inside the cab and the ear-battering monotony of the motor (which was far louder than it should have been as the vehicle lacked a muffler—Chris wore a device on her head that held padded cups against her ears to block out the sound), the novelty of my privileged perch soon wore off. The vague pictures of farmland and forest, punctuated by occasional slowings or stoppings in deference to infrequent traffic lights or gas stations, soon became a meaningless blur.

All this time, the truck's shadow wavered back and forth upon the road in front of us; toward the end of the day, however, we veered left off the highway onto a lesser road and ground slowly up a couple of long hills. At the top we burst forth onto a wide, open plateau that undulated in rigid, tawny waves beneath the golden rays of a lowering sun. Dark patches of rusty-looking conifers were scattered upon the landscape. There was still a fair amount of traffic on the road, but its character had changed: smaller vehicles were shabbier, more utilitarian and more often than not pickups; the large trucks no longer sported peacock colours and sleek-sided containers, but were fitted with crude open racks that bulged with tree carcasses. All these vehicles were plastered with mud, and I soon found out why. Chris slowed, there was a bump, and we began to lurch and wallow like a mired pig. The front end of the canoe jerked and groaned against its restraining ropes as it waggled back and forth.

The sun's uncompromising eye glared directly through the windshield. I compensated by turning my back on it, but Chris screwed her features into a rictus akin to that of agony in her efforts to stare it down. Soon, however, she also admitted defeat. The battering roar of the motor waned as the vehicle was coerced over some kind of potholed bush road, and it eventually coughed into blessed silence.

I sat up and stretched as much as my proximity to the ceiling would allow. I put on a questioning look: —*Are we there?* But all Chris took out of the truck was enough food for both of us for one night, our dishes and her bedroll, on which she sat while she lit a small fire in an old firepit full of gobs of half-melted, broken glass. Behind us stood a sparse straggle of short trees; in front, a small lake, still largely frozen. It sat like an icy pearl in its ring of tawny grass. Beyond it was the road along which the logging trucks droned and winked, never ceasing their thundering progress throughout the night. Our sleep was restless, and by the following morning, both Chris's sleeping bag and my grizzled coat were white with frost.

The sun had barely risen when we once more took our places in the vehicle. The openness of the landscape left us, and the rutted road became hedged by brittle-looking forest. Its composition was very different from the mix of sweeping cedars and firs I was used to; these trees simply went on and on, dwarfed, spiky, mean and uncompromising. Cloud began to infiltrate the sky, and I must have nodded off again, for as we pulled off the road a second time, it was apparent by the sun that several more hours had passed. This time, we drove into someone's yard.

I love visiting. I have heard it said that it takes 22 muscles in a human face to produce a frown and only half a dozen for a smile. Indeed, it is little effort to slide back one's ears and part one's lips into a grin, and wiggling my backside makes me feel good all over.

Not all humans are well-bred enough to greet a dog properly in return, but the woman who came out of the house gave me a pat and said, "What a neat little dog! Is it part wolfhound?"

"Oh no," laughed Chris. "Just a mutt."

I sighed to myself. I was always piqued at Chris's denigration of the classifications that were often afforded me. What harm would it have done to lay claim to wolfhound genes? It's not as though the other human had called me something ghastly like a cockapoo. And who knows? If it is impossible to authenticate wolfhound genes within my family tree, then it is equally impossible to refute them.

The other human, however, was not really a dog person (although I appreciated her attempts to be polite), and the conversation soon turned to other things. I became much more interested in the proceedings when Chris reversed the truck toward a shed and began to unload most of the gear. This building had obviously never been lived in, for it bore none of the usual effluvia associated with human dwellings.

—*Is this it then?* I wagged hopefully, as much to make conversation as anything else, for it did not seem a very comfortable place.

But Chris, as she off-loaded, wore the same expression that had soured her features when she had put her possessions onto the truck two days before. While she grunted and muttered and wrestled with the canoe, I tactfully busied myself with sniffing around. Both human and dog smells were faded, however, and the ground was clean and sweet with that rather unformed and immature scent of a land only recently bereft of snow. The rough road led past the house and dipped toward a lake—a much bigger one than where we had camped. This lake was also largely iced around its edges, and when I went down to get a drink from the open puddles by the shore, I noticed a strong oily aroma of some sort of fuel issuing from a tank under a nearby lean-to. It smelled almost like the gas Chris put into her truck, but not quite. Fuel not being high on my list of favourite smells, however, it failed to hold my interest.

Despite my examination of our surroundings, I had not failed to keep a watchful eye on my food dish—whither thou goeth, so will I. It had been taken out of the truck right away, but had been placed close by on the ground. Sure enough, once almost everything else had been removed, the dish and Chris's backpack were tossed back inside once more. I can't say I was altogether sorry; there was a rawness and a lack of refinement to the place that did not sit easily on my soul. Had I known what was to come, I would have looked at it with a different eye. In later years, this rough but friendly outpost would seem the very epitome of civilization.

Oddly enough, although the box in the back of the truck was now empty, I was still allowed to ride in the cab. And what unprecedented luxury that was! There were now no cartons in there, and I sat directly on the soft, springy seat. I could not see through the windows unless I sat up straight, but the hedonistic pleasure of my unusual position more than compensated for this deficit.

The road deteriorated further, and slowly we began to climb. Now there was very little traffic of any sort. The trees grew darker and changed to compact-shaped conifers with which I was unfamiliar; pockets of sour-looking willow swamp were bare-twigged and half-frozen, and soon we had regressed into winter. The road itself remained clear of snow, but its surface became one great, grabbing bog. The truck slewed and slithered and spat gobs of mud and gravel from its scrabbling tires. High, gravel-pocked banks of dirty ice lined the river of mud over which we drove. At one point, Chris stopped the truck and we got out. The country was rolling, rocky and sparsely forested. A thick, unbroken white blanket filled the spaces between the trees. It was very silent: no traffic, no bird, no wind, just the dull, implacable nothingness of snow. There were no animal tracks and few scents of anything at all. I shivered, and not only with the cold. This was an alien land, wild, stark and forbidding. I looked at my human's face for a clue; imagine my alarm on seeing Chris smile. It was a peculiar smile—not altogether friendly, more excited, savage even. It was a smile of triumph. Surely, I thought with great apprehension, this could not be *it*? To my enormous relief, Chris motioned me back into the truck, donned her ear protectors and once more began to drive.

And suddenly we were perched on the lip of a precipice with the land swooping in fast falls beneath us. Beyond the drop, enormous mountains rose. Grinding in low gear, the old truck inched tightly around tortured hairpin bends; soon a whiff of hot brake rubber leaked through the gaps around the ill-fitting, rust-holed door.

Down and down we went, and it was at this point that I first began to be visited by a curious feeling. Odd, vague images started to filter through my memory. I did not know it at the time, but I was experiencing small traces of déjà vu.

It must be remembered that I had left this country at a very young age; moreover, I had spent most of the journey away from it crouched in abject terror between boxes on the vehicle's floor. But as the switchbacks flipped us lower and lower, we moved dramatically from winter into spring. And just as the scents of a land newly released from winter's bondage assailed my nostrils, waves of recollection began to assault my mind.

The tree aromas changed; the wizened upper forest was transformed once more to familiar spruce, firs and cedars. "Ah! Smell the cottonwoods," Chris exclaimed as she snorted great gulps of a scent whose jolt to the sinuses quite frankly left me cold. (I have to admit that I find humans' olfactory preferences one of the more puzzling aspects of their makeup.) Nonetheless, it was the cottonwood balm that triggered more of the brain's memory, for these trees, I suddenly knew without a doubt, had surrounded the shack where I was born. It brought to mind the tangled companionship of my brothers and sisters, the hole in the ground, the old man who lived in the shack and, close by, the scent and the sound of a wild rushing river. Sure enough, slowly growing larger as we descended, there appeared a ribbon of white-foamed water roaring over broken beds of boulders. Along with the scents of snowmelt and a lingering, feral smell that was rather disturbing but which I could not quite identify, was the faint yet unmistakable and most delectable aroma of wonderfully rotted fish.

Had the truck been animate, its brakes would have sighed with relief once we got to the bottom of The Hill (as I later learned to call that great, plunging stretch of switchbacks). Once again we hit pavement and were soon bowling along merrily through a tunnel of tall, sweet, coastal forest. We slowed and pulled off onto another driveway; this one squeezed its way over body-thick roots between massive boles of fir. At the end was an open space with a log house on one side and, on the other, a scattering of cabins half-drowned in the sweeping fronds of cedars. Beyond was the kind of mountain vista that invariably inspires the human animal to exclamations of wonder and joy. As the truck belched to a stop, Chris gave the predictable "Wow!" and "Look at that, Lonesome" and then a singing "Hi, guys!" as two more humans exited the door of the house.

"Chris!" said the man. "You made it." And I prepared to do my greeting in my turn, but I had hardly leapt from the truck before a hideous barking ensued, and a wire-haired tan-coloured bitch rushed, raised-hackled and stiff-legged, from around the back of the house.

"Sally," roared the male human. But I was already bouncing from the back bumper bar over the tailgate of the truck; discretion, I am never slow to advise, is always the better part of valour. The strange female human laughed admiringly at my acrobatics, for the truck was tall, and not many dogs of my size could have achieved such a leap. It certainly put this "Sally" in her place, and I could sense that even though she continued to bark aggressively, she at once afforded me a modicum of respect.

Seeing that the situation seemed to be under control, the three humans went into the house and shut the door. At once, Sally calmed down, and we were able to have a much more civilized conversation in the kind of language dogs worldwide can understand.

With a curl of her lip, Sally intimated, —*Where have you come from?*

—*Salmon Arm*, I replied with a slumping of my shoulder, a gesture of definite subservience as was correct under the circumstances, but I was not going so far as to fawn abjectly; there are innumerable subtleties to this movement in dogspeak.

—*Must be quite a way. You smell very different from anyone I know around here.*

—*Two days*, I said modestly.

—*Hmm*, said Sally, allowing some of the stiffness to leave her tail. She eyed me circumspectly. —*You can come down if you like. I only do that routine because my humans like it.*

—*Thanks*, I said, hopping neatly over the tailgate again. We sniffed each other politely for a moment.

—*I travel quite a bit, too*, said Sally. —*Sometimes I spend days at a time in our van. We drive all the way back to Ontario some winters. Other times we go by plane.* She looked at me slyly. —*Bet you've never been in a plane.*

I was not, at that time, very sure what a plane was. But I had undoubtedly never been in one, and I dutifully drooped my head. Satisfied that she had gained a little in status, Sally relaxed further and we began to nose companionably at an old mouse smell in a clump of bushes. —*Come on, I'll show you the garden*, said my host after a moment. —*Who else is in your pack?* She asked this quite casually as we trotted round the corner of the house. I was slightly behind her so she could not see my expression; however, she caught my hesitation and turned back toward me.

—*Er, no one*, I replied, looking embarrassed. —*My human seems to prefer it that way.* I managed to convey, by a lift of an eyebrow, that I most heartily disapproved of this situation but was far too loyal to ever actually admit it.

—*Ah*, said Sally sympathetically. —*A spinster.* She glanced at the vehicle. —*Doesn't look like the gushy sort, though. Is she strict?*

—*She's something of a disciplinarian*, I replied carefully. A termagant, I thought to myself darkly.

Sally chuckled. —*I see. No treats at the table and no sleeping on the bed. That kind, eh?*

I nodded ruefully.

—*My pack's a couple with a little boy, a grandma and a cat. They spoil me quite a bit.* Then she sighed. —*But I don't get to sleep on the bed either, as my female human is allergic to dog dandruff. Still, I lead a pretty good life on the whole. I have A Purpose, and that's always gratifying.*

—*Oh?* I offered politely, wondering what was coming. We had arrived at the compost heap, and I sniffed it hopefully but found it surprisingly devoid of interesting smells.

—*Yes*, said Sally proudly. —*A Purpose. And that*, she added shrewdly, *is why you're getting so little feedback through your nose at this point.*

I turned to her, puzzled and not a little ashamed that she had so easily read my thoughts.

—*Bears*, she said succinctly.

My eyes rounded.

—*Bears*, said Sally again, grinning a little and letting her tongue flop out from between her teeth. —*My job is to warn the humans when bears are about, especially when the little boy is playing in the yard.*

Bears! my mind screamed. I knew at once that this was the origin of the feral aroma that had greeted me when we were driving down The Hill and that was still present in the olfactory background. I tried to remain outwardly nonchalant. —*Um, do you get a lot of them?* I asked, in as bored a tone as I could manage.

—*Tons*, said Sally, grinning wolfishly. —*Black bears and grizzlies. They feed on those dandelions in that meadow below the garden.* I peered nervously over the bank, but the meadow lay blandly empty except for a million golden blossoms. —*And that's why the pack is so careful about what they put in the compost heap. They daren't put anything in it that a bear might like. Every bear treat is kept*

39

in locked buildings. Food, garbage . . . even my kibble is kept shut up in the house. Salmon Arm, where you come from, must be like Ontario. No one knows anything about bears there either. You a city dog, then?

—*Not really city*, said I, thinking of Snoopy and my scathing assessment of his inability to climb through fences, but feeling, nonetheless, somewhat out of my depth in this place. —*Actually, we lived on a farm.* All at once, I decided to confide in her, liking her despite her gruffness. —*As a matter of fact, I was born somewhere around here.*

—*Were you really?* said Sally, at once greatly interested. —*I know pretty well all the families in these parts. What was your maiden name?*

—*Unfortunately, I don't remember. I was taken away at a very young age and have only the dimmest memories of where I was born.*

—*Me too*, said Sally. —*Taken away early, that is. But I used to see some of my birth-pack members sometimes, even my mother once in a while, although come to think of it, I haven't seen any of them now for a while. Their human comes here fairly often. He's a male and quite ancient. He's got a pickup even more beat-up than yours, although his is smaller.*

—*I seem to recall that my birth-pack human was also an old male. I don't remember any other human living with him. In fact, now that I think of it, my current human was only the second one I can ever remember seeing.*

—*Same as me!* Sally laughed. —*But there's a fair number of old guys living alone in this part of the world. Do you remember anything else?*

—*There were . . . things keep coming back to me; it's extraordinary how that happens—I do believe there were a large number of cats. Black ones.*

Me and my long-lost sister . . . Chris had brought me home.

Sally stopped short in mid-snuff and looked at me.

—*How old are you?* she said suddenly, and there was a curious cast to her voice.

—*A bit over a year.*

—*Did the man, by any chance*, said Sally, scratching her ear thoughtfully with a hind foot, —*have a long white beard?*

I glanced at her sharply. An untoward excitement began to grow. —*You know*, I panted excitedly, —*I do believe he did.*

—*My Dog!* said Sally. —*I don't believe this! You've gotta be Runty!*

I sat back on my heels in amazement.

—*You're right*, I said. —*I'd forgotten my maiden name until you said it. Now it's all coming back to me. You mean—you mean you knew us?*

—*Not only knew you*, said Sally, grinning from ear to ear, —*I'm from the same litter. Tan Sister. That's my real name. Don't you remember me?*

I stared at her in utter astonishment. Tan Sister! —*Well of course I remember you. You were the first . . . And this is where you . . . Wow! I don't believe this! You're my long-lost sister!* And the two of us were so delighted with this discovery that we started to tear around the yard with the abandon of a couple of pups who'd found a discarded beer can with its contents still intact. Later, when my human emerged from the house and drew her pack and the food dishes from the truck, my happiness was complete. All the packing and snappishness and the long, long journey had been made with a purpose after all.

Chris had brought me home.

CHAPTER FOUR

BUT—AH, BUT. IT WAS STILL not the end of the journey.

A few days later, to my utter chagrin, the backpack, the dog dish, Chris and I were once more relegated to the truck. The humans pantomimed their farewell rituals, and I gave Tan Sister a brief wag before doing my trick over the tailgate, not, it must be said, without a modicum of vanity. Tan Sister, however, simply turned her nose away and affected a bored look. The truck went through its choking-raven routine—"You gotta pump the hell out of it," Chris yelled over the racket to her bemused friends—but eventually it coughed its throat clear and spluttered and banged into life. Slowly we wobbled along the tree-hung driveway and turned once more onto the road.

For a short while we retraced our steps up the valley. I began to wonder if the place where we had left Chris's monumental pile of impedimenta was to be our home after all. But just before we started to climb the switchbacks of The Hill, we veered onto another bush track, all but concealed, which proved to be the absolute worst substrate we had hitherto driven over. For the most part, the track stuck close to the river. It had to, for a great wall of rock slides and bluffs reared straight up the other side. The truck crashed and banged over boulders that had fallen from these; it sloshed through rushing creeks; it squeezed over crude bridges whose decks were often only two planks—one for each wheel. I was thrown around in the truck box like flotsam in a storm; my legs ached with the effort of balancing. I tried to sit, I tried to stand, but the moment I thought I had mastered the rhythm, I was tossed into a corner again. "Sorry, Lonesome," Chris would bellow through the sliding windows at the back of the cab after a particularly bad bump. I could see by the way she was hunched over the wheel that she was not enjoying the drive either.

For all that, there was something invigorating about the journey. The air smelled soft and moist; the cottonwoods and aspens wore misty veils of green; eagles spiralled against the tops of the bluffs; and the river, always the river, rolled and sang boisterously along its rocky bed beneath us.

And then we came, with no prior warning, to a clearing.

Not just any clearing, but *the* clearing.

It hit me like a thunderclap.

It was the place where I was born.

But no tall old bearded man sat upon the stoop of a cabin; no little puppies tumbled about the yard. Even the shack was gone. All that remained in the clean sweep of the grassy meadow that stretched between the river and the road was an area of hard-worn earth within which, still distinct, was the shape of a square. In the middle of the square was a crumbling hollow. This, then, was all that was left of my natal home. I would have appreciated time to read the messages among the scents of earth and grass and river to try to piece together a few more clues to my ancestral history, but Chris never even stopped. With a lurch and bump, the clearing was behind us.

Suddenly, an enormous animal dived onto the road. At first glance, it was vaguely horse-like, but it was huge. Its feet were split, like a cow's, but longer, and they struck out in a great, kicking trot. A hump graced the animal's shoulders, and it appeared to have been

44

subjected to the hideous practice that many humans inflict upon us canines: having its tail docked in infancy. In some respects it vaguely resembled the mule deer that sometimes flitted around the farm where I had spent my childhood, but it was far larger, and its horns were horizontal poles with knobs on the ends that stuck out on either side of its head. It did not look at all friendly, but I hardly had time to register it before it had pounded off the road and into the forest.

A short while after this encounter, we staggered to a stop. The choking raven died, and the usual blessed aural relief ensued. Into the vacuum filtered a motley collection of birdsong and the nearby growl of the river. A smaller creek tumbled from the mountains to our left. Across the creek was a footbridge that was far too narrow to accommodate the truck.

"Okay, Lonesome," said Chris, and there was an underlying excitement to her voice. "This is where we start walking."

Walk? Thank Dog! I thought, leaping gratefully out of the truck box. Out of the cab came the backpack, which was bulging a fair amount, I noted, as it did when we were going to be out for a night or two. Chris laced up her boots. She stood for a moment, smiling and sniffing the air; then we were off.

Any kind of walk was an adventure in those days. The ever-present effluvium of bear could not be ignored, but it was distant; I was young, and I still had no notion of what the future held. My spirits rose; the other scents of the forest were enticing, and there was a jaunty skip to my stride as I trotted on ahead.

The trail was well used by all sorts of animals, including humans. Most of the people smells, however, were from the previous summer; there was something rather daring about the thought of being amongst the first hikers to set foot here this year. For the most part, the path kept close to the river; sometimes we crunched noisily over gravel-strewn rocky bluffs hanging precariously over the boiling rapids; sometimes we slipped like ghosts through dark cedar forests where our feet made no sound in the deep brown duff. After a while, we came to a lake that sat like a blue eye within the steep walls of the valley. At its foot, the trail crossed the river on a bridge and began to climb up the other side.

I trotted right along, noting the sudden sharp musky smell of a weasel-like creature, but I suddenly realized that Chris was not following me. She had forsaken the footpath and had begun to force her way through the scrub along the lakeshore. —*Hey*, I panted. —*The trail's this way. Can't you see?* But Chris (as she is so often wont to do) ignored me completely. There was no logic at all to her caprice, but in this instance, as in so many others, there was nothing I could do to make her change her mind.

So around the lake we went. It was not at all easy. When we were not forcing our way through brush, we were teetering from boulder to boulder on rock slides. The lake had not looked very big from the outlet, but it took Chris quite a while to force her way round it. (I, needless to say, unburdened and much shorter-legged, managed it a great deal more easily.)

—*You see*, I said with my eyebrows, pulling them into a small frown of gentle chastisement, —*wouldn't the trail have been a great deal more comfortable?*

But as the lake ended, we plunged again into a cedar forest and picked up another trail. Everything might have been all right, except now I had something else to worry me. This part was downright scary. For it was here that the bear smell became so strong that it could no longer be ignored.

It's not that a bear's scent is particularly unpleasant, and at that point in my life I had never actually met one of the animals. I had little real idea of what kind of creatures they were beyond the snippets of reputation I had gleaned. But there was something about the aroma that struck shivers up my spine. This, moreover, was no casual perfume wafted on a passing breeze or hint of an ancient scent against a marking tree, but an odour that spoke unmistakably of the animals' immediate presence. No more trotting and sniffing and running round in circles; I kept tight against Chris's heels. I was convinced there were eyes watching us from behind every tree, and my head was screwed around over my shoulder as I walked. Chris strode along as though she had no care in the world. (I have mentioned, I believe, how poorly developed was her sense of smell.) Every time she stopped to examine a plant (which was a peculiar, sheep-like habit of hers, although she only occasionally grazed any of them), I was concentrating so hard on the world behind us that I always bumped into her legs.

"Oh, Lonesome," Chris laughed after I had collided with her for the umpteenth time. "Just look at your tail jammed between your legs. I wouldn't have thought a dog's tail could be shoved so far forward."

—*Huh*, I muttered grumpily. —*I'd just like to see what your tail would do if you knew for a fact that there was a bear right behind that very boulder.*

And yet, despite the proximity of a number of ursine animals of all ages and sizes, we never actually saw one of them. And after a while, the forest opened out again and, to my great relief, the intensity of the bear scent diminished.

But hardly had I got over that fright when a new one was presented to me. The sound of the river had accompanied us all the way, even though we did not always walk beside it. At this point, it had split into several branches, each singing its different song through the forest. However, a brasher roaring began to gain strength as we marched along. All of a sudden we topped a stony bank and found ourselves confronted with a wildly crashing creek cutting straight across our path. All the previous creeks we had faced had been bridged, albeit crudely, but there didn't seem to be any kind of aid to crossing the water here. Chris looked upstream, she looked downstream—and then, to my horror, stepped right in. Instantly her leg was swallowed to the knee, the water piling against it with little licks of foam. She staggered, steadied herself and followed with the other foot. Swaying and lurching, she reeled across, then heaved herself clumsily out on the far side.

"Come on, Lonesome," she called. She plonked herself onto a rock, unlaced her boots and began to wring out her socks.

—*Come on?* I gasped. —*You can't be serious. It's horribly dangerous, and it's **wet**.* I sat and looked at her.

Splish splatter, went the water from her socks, audible even above the river's roar. She began to pull on her boots.

"Lonesome," she sang, in what was obviously an attempt to imitate her dinnertime tone of voice.

But I was not fooled. Apart from the falsehood in the tone, dinnertime it definitely was not. And I knew full well that, hard taskmaster though she was, she would never leave me alone in a place like this.

But she got up, hauled on her backpack and began to walk away.

I couldn't believe it. She was abandoning me! I screamed, —*You can't leave me. You can't leave me.*

"Why, Lonesome," called Chris a little crossly, raising her voice above the crash of water, "I haven't heard you make a noise like that since you were a puppy. Come on. You can do it."

Then she pushed through some bushes and was gone.

Unbidden, a vision of Snoopy's pathetic bemusement at trying to figure out his first fence flooded into my mind. Any other human would have taken pity on the beginner and gone back to show him the way. But Chris had simply abandoned him and left him to work things out for himself. Now she was doing the same to me.

But this was no mere fence rail.

This was the water monster incarnate.

This was The Wet.

Desperately, I put a paw into the water.

The current whipped at it—and it was icy cold. I dragged it out.

Frantically, I ran up and down the bank, yelping uselessly. Chris was out of sight; I was alone.

—*Don't leave me, Chris. Don't leave me!*

What to do? Should I run back to Tan Sister? Could I find my way? I looked again at The Wet. There was a boulder just breaking the surface a few steps into the maelstrom. If I jumped, I could probably reach it. And from there, perhaps I could make the next one. The longer I thought about it, the scarier the idea got. If I thought about it for too long, I would never be able to do it.

So I leapt. Bounded from one rock to the other.

I was over!

And I didn't even get my feet wet.

I tore along the path and bumped right into Chris, who had been waiting for me just out of sight.

"There, Lonesome. I knew you could do it. Good girl." My confidence returned with a rush, and I capered joyfully to be reunited with the only pack I had. And in truth, I began to feel inordinately pleased at the way I had managed to foil the water monster; my only regret was that Tan Sister had not been there to witness my bravery.

Not far past this creek, we came to another lake. This one was the biggest we had so far seen; it marched on past several plummeting bluffs and was backed by a distant, snow-laden peak.

"There you are, Lonesome," said Chris. "This is Lonesome Lake. This is what you were named after."

I gazed at the water with considerable surprise. Me? Named after a lake? What an extraordinary idea to name a dog after a whole bunch of *Wet*. And why this lake? A small portent of alarm began to niggle away at my consciousness. What could this mean?

We had been travelling for the better part of the day by now, and Chris decided to make a camp. It was a calm, soft evening. The still, mild air carried scents of deer, mice, the peculiar humped animal with the docked tail that we had met on the road and bear, although the last, thank goodness, was less threatening here. There were olfactory traces of people, also. They were old and faint, but at least it meant that someone had been here before us. We weren't completely beyond the reach of civilization. As I turned three times on a nice springy patch of crunchy old cottonwood leaves, I hung onto that thought and found it enormously comforting.

Scrambling round this second lake was in part a repetition of the first, but there were traces of a trail in places, which helped quite a bit. Toward its end, the trail suddenly became wide and distinct again, and to my delight it was overlaid with more recent human aroma. However, as we plunged into the forest once more, the country seemed as wild and harsh as ever. Imagine my enormous amazement, therefore, when we suddenly stumbled upon a fence. Beyond were the smells of domestic animals: cows, horses, chickens and cats; overlaying it all were the fresh odours of woodsmoke, cooked meat and living, breathing human beings. Chris pushed open a heavy, creaky wooden gate; we walked across a fenced grassy field dotted with old log buildings and came to a house. There was a garden fence made of slim, upright poles, and a small gate with a bell that rang as we opened it, followed by the heavy thump of boots on a wooden floor. The door of the house opened and two people stood there, waiting for Chris to approach.

They were both quite a bit older than Chris. They were short and powerful with strong, capable-looking hands. Their clothes were drab with hard use, and they wore the comfortable air of being monarchs of all they surveyed—as indeed they were, I was to find out later. These two people had created everything human-made in sight—the fences, barns, fields, gardens, bridges and most of their tools. They had made everything from the original swath of forest that had completely covered the valley, with no help from anyone except their horses and their cows.

The couple was well mannered and reserved, exhibiting none of the usual emotional parodies so favoured by most humans of my acquaintance, and I felt at home with them at once. Chris shucked her pack and disappeared inside the house. I could smell bread and meat and pickles, so I knew they were about to eat. I had long ago become used to smelling food while being forced to abstain and was, moreover, pretty tired after the physical and emotional strain of the last couple of days; thus I was happy enough to curl up on the porch and have a little snooze. There were no bear smells at all close to the house, and for the first time since leaving Tan Sister's place, I began to relax.

All of a sudden, a black, prick-eared head popped up from behind a nearby clump of grass. Languid jaws rimmed with tiny sharp white teeth opened in a prodigious red yawn. It was a cat.

—*Hullo*, I said, sliding my ears forward in polite surprise. I had been astonished at one point in my career to learn that many dogs chase cats. But I could see no point in being anything other than civil to these less fortunate beings, although I find cats in general to be rather uninteresting. I've never seen them do anything useful, and I admit to some puzzlement as to why humans persist in having them around their houses. This one was carrying its self-absorption to the point of being downright rude; my polite soft whine and gentle tail wag were simply ignored.

There was a scrape of chairs from inside the house, and the building trembled faintly as three heavy pairs of boots renewed their contact with the floor.

"We'll take you over there and you can have a look," the woman was saying as she opened the door. (Even the latch was wooden; how mellifluous is the sound of wood sliding against wood compared with the harsh metallic clatter of most door fastenings.)

"There's one of your cats," said Chris. "Oh," she added curiously, "do you keep it tied?"

And then I saw what I had failed to notice before: that the cat wore a collar, like many dogs I knew, and this was fastened by a light chain to a small tree. No wonder the poor creature was standoffish. On the rare occasions I had been similarly restrained, it had been as a punishment of such great magnitude (vis-à-vis the time I had ended up in the pound) that I had been consumed with mortification. What on earth, I thought, might this cat have done to deserve such unconscionable treatment?

"We tie all our cats during the day in the summer," the man explained. "They don't seem to mind. The idea is to try to keep them from catching birds. But it's amazing. The birds fly right down in front of the cats' noses while they sit there, so they still get 'em. You'd think the birds would have more sense."

I'd had little to do with birds, but I was not at all surprised to hear this. As a pup, I'd wondered for a while if the squeaky noises and fluttery movements they made were an invitation to play, but they, like cats, had exhibited a supreme indifference to my overtures. And the neighbour's chickens (which, although they do not look much like it, are indeed a kind of bird) had been regarded with such contempt that they had been caged. No, when brains and charisma were handed out in this world, birds received a pretty poor allotment, that's for sure.

So the cat, then, was to be ignored, like any other criminal. I had no problem with that and happily followed the three humans on their walk.

Angling away from the house, we came to yet another creek. This was actually part of the main river that had slid away on some business of its own for a while as so often seemed to happen in this valley. I was enormously relieved to see that it had been bridged.

But the bridge was unlike any I had ever seen before. It consisted merely of two thin logs placed high above the stream; the logs were reached by climbing up a split-cedar ramp. (There were no sawn boards on the place; as I have said before, everything was homemade.) The two thin logs were narrow and bouncy, and they wobbled precariously as the humans placed their weight upon them. Determinedly, I followed, but the swiftly moving river coruscated in a disorienting way as it whirled beneath the uneven gap between the logs. I concentrated hard on placing my feet, keeping my paws unnaturally apart, both right paws on one log, and the left ones on the other. I was considerably relieved to be able to leap off the other side.

A moment or two later, we came to another bridge. This one spanned the main part of the river, but it was a far better specimen. It was wide and solid and paved with small logs and more split-cedar

We crossed several creeks, and I was enormously relieved to find any that had been bridged.

boards; had there been a road up to it, it would have been possible to drive Chris's truck across. Having negotiated a gate at the far end, we turned upstream a little ways, and then the humans fell to talking.

"The river's still low," Chris's friend was saying. "Those gravel bars are covered up in the flood."

"We scattered grass seed around here, but nothing seemed to grow, which is why we can let you have it," said the woman. "Most of our quarter section is useless land from a farming point of view. It goes way up this side of the valley through all those rocks and bluffs. It's been quite a struggle finding pockets of productivity that will grow enough feed for our livestock. We can't afford to let any fertile land be wasted."

"Looks fine to me," Chris said. "It's got a fabulous view across the river to that mountain up there, and I love the way the river twists around the bend upstream and roars around the island." She examined the alders that fringed the river. "You're much later up here, I see. Down at Stuie" (which is what humans called Tan Sister's place), "the leaves are already coming out, but they're still a long way from opening this far up the river."

"Yes, we're quite a bit later," the woman acquiesced. "About a month, I'd guess." Her voice was low and unstressed and it slid as smoothly as gentle water rippling over stones.

"We'll be taking the birch for firewood," said the man, equally quietly. "There's not much left on the property, and we like to barbecue meat a lot; fir and cedar are no good for that because of the resin."

A sharp rapping noise issued from said birch, and from around the trunk came a small red-headed woodpecker tapping hopefully at a neatly stitched row of holes.

"Yellow-bellied sapsucker," Chris said with satisfaction. Unlike me, she took an interest in avian activities.

"You'd better camp well away from any trees you might be falling," advised the man. "We've picked out another spot for you where you won't damage any grass."

And with that, we headed back downstream, passed the bridge and walked a little ways upon the bank. From here, more of the farm was visible: the barn, the chicken house and the large fenced rectangle of the garden.

"We had to build the fences seven feet tall, with rails no more than six inches apart," said the woman, noticing Chris's gaze. "Otherwise the deer jump over or wriggle through and eat our food. We can't afford to feed the wildlife when it takes so much work to grow what we need for ourselves."

"And we've brought you this camping stove over," said the man, indicating a rusted metal box on legs. "It gets pretty windy here sometimes, and it's not a good idea to have unprotected fires. We can't risk a forest fire."

"It looks fabulous," said Chris, referring to the location; she was eyeing the dented stove with some misgivings. But there was an undercurrent of excitement in her voice that I would have done well to take more notice of. I, however, had become distracted by that interesting weasely smell I'd encountered before; this was even stronger. Suddenly a much larger cousin of the animal with which I was familiar ran along the stones at the edge of the river. Its coat was dark, but it ran with the same looping delicacy before slipping out of sight beneath a log.

"There's a mink," said the man.

"Oh, so there is," said Chris. "You know," she began a little awkwardly, "it's so wonderful to be in a place where wild animals still live a normal life. There are so few places left like that in the world."

But I sensed that Chris was trying to say more and didn't really know how. This was unusual, for she is generally a fairly gabby creature. There was a small silence.

"You can come and get some milk if you want," said the woman. "And we'll give you a couple of jars of meat to get started."

"I really appreciate all this," said Chris. "It's going to be a wonderful experience."

"I expect it will be," allowed the man.

On our way back to the house, we had, needless to say, to cross the two bridges. The first, of course, was no problem at all. The second presented me with an obstacle I had not bargained for. The two wobbly poles had been distasteful enough on their own, but as we had come across the first time, I had leapt down with such alacrity that I had given no thought as to how we were going to get back onto them again. For this end was much farther above the ground than the other had been, and, unlike the other, it was not serviced by a ramp. The only way to climb up was via a vertical five-runged ladder built of poles.

Up went the humans while I sat, nonplussed, at the bottom. *What on earth do they expect of me now? —Hey*, I yelled. *—What about me?*

"Lonesome," expostulated Chris, exasperated. "The water's only six inches deep, for goodness' sake."

—I don't care, I stormed belligerently. *—It's wet.*

The other woman chuckled. It was the first time I had seen her laugh. "She's not very brave, is she?"

"You ought to have seen her coming across Hunlen Creek," Chris guffawed. "She yelled like a stuck pig until she figured out she could leap from rock to rock and get over that way. And yet Sally, the littermate that Michael and Debbie have down at Stuie, adores water and flings herself in the river any chance she gets. Debbie and Michael tell me she swims for miles behind their canoe when they're back in Ontario."

Nonetheless, Chris came back to me, climbed down the ladder and lifted me onto the poles.

No way! I thought to myself. I'm simply going to stay over on this side. Before she had climbed up again, I had jumped off.

"Oh forget it, Lonesome." Now Chris was cross. "If that's the way you want it." And she climbed back up the ladder in order to follow her disappearing friends.

I could hardly believe she was doing this to me again. On top of which, the unfavourable comparison to Tan Sister had stung me to the quick. I wanted nothing to do, however, with The Wet. Quick as a flash, I hooked my paws over the poles and scrambled up the ladder, tight against Chris's heels.

"Well I'll be darned," said Chris. She was gratifyingly amazed. "Dogs're not supposed to be able to climb ladders. You're not so dumb after all. But you really are a funny little creature. I've never seen another dog go to such lengths to keep her feet dry."

And why else, I thought grumpily, do you wear boots? But I was pleased, not only to have been so easily forgiven for my transgressions, but also for managing to do something that merited a measure of praise. And yet, as far as I was concerned, climbing ladders was a piece of Milk-Bone compared to dealing with water monsters. Chris was really extraordinarily obtuse at times.

Quick as a flash, I hooked my paws over the poles and scrambled up the ladder.

CHAPTER FIVE

CAMPING WAS SOMETHING CHRIS AND I had done quite often, so spending a couple of nights beside the river did not seem so extraordinary. Chris set up the little tin stove that the homesteaders had given her, supporting the chimney by tying wires around it and guying them to encircling trees. Beside it she erected her little backpacking tent. While she was doing this, I kept a sharp nose out for the mink, but although I caught its acrid scent several times, I did not see it again. Squirrels rustled noisily through the spring-dry remnants of last year's fallen leaves, and a pair of sharp-billed mergansers bobbed swiftly on the current downriver. As it grew dark, Chris crouched close to the stove, for the temperature dropped below freezing once the sun went behind the mountain.

The following day, Chris did a lot of idle walking about and muttering to herself; she stood and looked at trees from every angle or sat for long periods by the river with a dreamy look on her face. But it was the strengthening light of dawn that brought out her most rapturous expostulations. "What a pity you can't see that gorgeous pink colour!" she exclaimed to me as the sunlight worked its way down the mountain.

—*Big deal!* I retorted grumpily into my moustache. —*What a pity you can't smell mouse.* A morning person I definitely am not.

I was still in the dark about my fate—young animals rarely listen properly to what is being said—so when, on the third morning,

Chris picked up her backpack and trotted back over the bridges (both of which I could now negotiate with one paw tied behind my back), called goodbye to the homesteaders and started back along the path in the direction of the truck, I naturally assumed we were going home. I was not a little displeased when Chris insisted that I stay behind her on the trail instead of running around at my own whim. The homesteaders had told her it was safer when bears were around. Whereas this might well have been the case when these animals were in front of us, it meant Chris messed up the olfactory signals of all the animals, not just the bears, and that took quite a lot of fun out of the walk. But obedience is my code and as natural to me as breathing; I would no more have thought of disobeying my human than I would have voluntarily dived into The Wet. Instead, I consoled myself with the pleasure I would have recounting my adventures to Tan Sister. Surely her plane ride (whatever it was) could not have been as exciting as this.

When she is not just puttering about, Chris has the capacity to walk in a steady lope for long periods without a rest. As we started the day with just that pace, I was somewhat surprised when she halted while the morning was still young. We had hiked the trail to Lonesome Lake and gone around it for only a very short distance when, without any explanation, Chris slipped off her pack and sat on a log.

It was a glorious morning. The sky was cloudless and the sun was shining, but owing to the great height of the valley wall to the east, its rays had not yet reached us, and the air was still cool and sweet. A multitude of trills and warbles announced the spring business of the birds, some of which swam peacefully upon the mirror of the lake. At the point where we had stopped, a rough shed had been built; in front of it two logs jutted into the water. They were anchored by rocks at the shore end, and they sported a rough deck of split-cedar boards where they pushed out into the lake.

After a short while, I heard a vehicle. Ha! I thought happily. Visitors! And I jumped up to look around. But then I stopped short. The road had ended a whole day's walk away at the place where we had left the truck. How on earth could a vehicle get here?

Chris had also risen to her feet. She was shading her eyes with her hand and peering into the sun, which had just managed to clear the eastern mountains. "There's the plane, Lonesome."

—*Plane?* I panted dubiously. —*What . . . ? Where . . . ?*

The motor sound grew louder—and then I saw it: a dot the same size and hue as a ladybug, wobbling precariously far above the valley's rim. I blinked my eyes in disbelief. What was this? A mosquito with an unfortunate case of flatulence? Some kind of a purring eagle?

But the creature was swooping downward and rapidly growing larger; all of a sudden it hit The Wet in a fountain of spray, shattering the pristine morning mirror, and wallowed to a stop like an enormous duck. My Dog! I thought. It's a flying truck. But it was like no other truck I had ever seen. Two enormous rigid arms sprouted from the top of the cab, and the body of the vehicle was held well clear of the water by insect-thin legs. These culminated in the most extraordinary sausage-shaped feet, and as the truck chugged toward us, they pushed twin waves in front of them. What, I wondered, with no little thrill of apprehension, will the water monster think about that?

As it drew closer, I became utterly amazed. For strapped to one of its legs was Chris's canoe.

"Hi, Pete," said Chris, grinning at the man inside as she grasped a rope and secured the vehicle to the wharf. I waggled my rear end, but the driver barely noticed me, and I felt so vulnerable perched on the narrow, uneven decking, surrounded on all sides by The Wet, that I soon trotted back to the safety of the shore. As I did so, there was a loud *smack!* and when I turned around, the canoe had been flipped onto its back and was floating on the water. What a different animal it had become! No longer was it belligerent and gauche, sluggish and uncompromising. Now it was as nervy as a tuft of thistledown; if Chris had not swiftly caught its lead and secured it to a bush, it would have happily skittered away.

But only when the driver of this extraordinary flying truck commenced the next stage of the operations did it finally begin to dawn on me that life was not all it had hitherto seemed to be. For, resting in the cab, jammed and piled and filling every available space, were more objects that I instantly recognized. They were the packages, boxes, bags and rolls that Chris had unloaded from our truck in that strange, raw, windy high country, before we had come down The Hill.

To my initial puzzlement, then growing apprehension, the driver handed them to Chris one by one, and she stacked them in precarious heaps on the wharf. At the very last came items that caused my spirits to sink as low as they could go, for they confirmed, once and for all, the suspicions I had entertained. The last three commodities were large paper sacks. They were of a kind with which I was perfectly familiar, for they were filled with dog kibble. I had never seen so much food in one place at any one time.

And now the awful truth became clear to me. We weren't going home to Tan Sister or, indeed, anywhere else. We were going to stay right here. In this wild, uninhabited, lonely, bear-infested wilderness. And, judging by the amount of dog food that had been unloaded, we were going to stay here for a very, very long time.

My Dog! I thought. It's a flying truck.

The plane chugged away, then slowly began to turn. (Had Tan Sister really ridden in a thing like that—and all the way to Ontario?) It paused—and then suddenly bellowed forth with a battering noise like a giant woodpecker from hell. Chris's old truck, sans muffler, sang a veritable lullaby compared with this racket. The volume of sound was so immense that it hurt my ears and shook the very ground upon which we stood. The water monster was not going to like this, I thought, and I was right. A tremendous battle ensued. The water monster flung its tentacles about the plane's feet, and the plane shouted back in return. But gradually, the plane began to win. Faster and faster it travelled, and suddenly it was able to pull free. Once it was airborne, it flew rapidly back toward the valley rim, becoming eagle-sized, ladybug-sized, flea-sized and then disappearing.

And we were left with the small waves slapping irritatedly against the shore, grumbling about losing their fight, the pile of freight squatting mutely on the wharf, and the nervy, jittery canoe tugging fretfully against its leash.

The cessation of noise was at least some kind of relief, but unbelievably, yet another terror was in store for me. It is indeed a blessing that we have little idea as to what the future holds; otherwise, were it not for the necessity of emptying our bladders, I doubt any of us would ever trouble to get out of bed in the morning.

Chris scrambled over to the canoe and grasped it by its tether. I thought she was going to chastise it for its capricious display of bad manners—after all, she had, in no uncertain terms, let it know what she thought of it when it did not want to be placed on top of the truck. But instead, she exhibited a curious abasement, as if the boat had some kind of power over her, and she tugged it quite solicitously until it lay against the wharf. Next, she told me to *Sit* and *Stay*. At the best of times, these words make me feel as though I have received a slap in the face with a wet towel; they are particularly offensive when I know I have done nothing wrong. After I had somewhat grudgingly obeyed, to my utter shock she crooned to the thing and hopped inside. And at once she floated away from the wharf and— horror of horrors!—submitted herself to the embrace of the water monster.

I panicked. Obedience was forgotten. Dignity went out the window. I ran up and down the shore, howling like one demented.

"Lonesome! For goodness' sake shut up!" Chris roared.

—*Not until you come and get me*, I screamed.

I now know that Chris had never been in a canoe before, and she was simply worried about it tipping over. She had imagined that I would make it more difficult for her by leaping about and over-turning the boat. But once she had found that her own equilibrium was more predictable than she had at first envisioned, she scooted the canoe back to the wharf. She grasped the end of one of the logs and pulled her end of the canoe against it, then nosed the other close to the shore.

"Come on, then, Lonesome," she said. "Jump in."

—*What, me? Get in that thing? You must be out of your tree!*

I eyed the boat with considerable apprehension. But Chris was in there, and she seemed happy enough. The pod-like shell did not seem to be angering the water monster, and there was no actual Wet inside. I carefully reached out a paw and placed it on the canoe's narrow rim.

"No! Not that way, Lonesome," Chris shouted in alarm. "That won't work."

I placed the other foot beside it.

"Lonesome! Get back! I can't hold you," Chris cried. And then she started to laugh.

And a dreadful thing occurred. The nose of the boat slowly began to slide away from the wharf. Which would have been no problem at all had it not taken my front feet with it. Unfortunately, my back feet were still anchored to the log.

Too late, I tried to get back onto solid land, but the more I pushed with my front feet, the farther away from the wharf the boat wobbled. Wider and wider grinned the water monster beneath my ever-stretching belly. Chris was guffawing hopelessly now, but I assure you, what happened next was far from funny.

Perlop!

And the water monster smothered me with its cold, wet hands.

I bobbed up at once and scrambled immediately onto the rocks beside the shore. I shook myself to get rid of the water in my coat, then tore around in circles to get warm.

Chris was calling me again. "Come here," she said authoritatively, and I recognized the familiar beginnings of impatience in her voice. I stood uncertainly on the wharf, absolutely positive that I was never going to have anything to do with that canoe again. But Chris had angled the boat a little differently; this time she and I were within touching distance. "Come on," she wheedled, and she stretched a friendly hand toward me. You'd think I would have recognized that tone of voice by now and jumped well out of the way. But while I stood wavering in indecision, Chris made a sudden grab. Before I could say Jack Russell, she had grasped my front paws and dragged me right in!

I flopped awkwardly into the bottom of the boat and at once tried to scramble back out.

"Siddown," Chris yelled. The water monster batted us back and forth. "Sit!" bellowed Chris. "Or I'll dump you over the side."

Whether it was the threat that finally penetrated or a vestige

So this is what the world looks like when you are a duck!

of my innate obedience that took over, I am no longer sure. But, terrified though I was, I sat.

"Lie down, Lonesome! Lie down!"

Reluctantly, with great care, I did so.

And, believe it or not, the water monster calmed down.

Actually, once I got used to it, being in the canoe wasn't at all unpleasant. The sun was warm, Chris was no longer separated from me, and I began to relax. For a while I propped my chin on one of the thwarts and gazed about me, quite struck by my new perspective on life. So this is what the world looks like when you are a duck!

We were propelled by Chris's rhythmic use of a broad stick, and the motion was far more comfortable than anything I had ever endured in the truck. It was also a great deal quieter. The water birds murmured; a little fish plopped. I began to grow drowsy; it was not long before I curled into a ball and fell asleep.

CHAPTER SIX

THE NEXT THING ON CHRIS'S self-imposed agenda was to move her possessions to the campsite. First they were put into the canoe and paddled over The Wet. I ran along the shore. I didn't relish being separated from Chris like that, but as long as she stayed close to the edge of the water, I did not mind so much. Soon all the boxes and bags were stashed at the head of the lake, and George and Kathleen (these were the names the homesteaders went by) and two other members of their pack, Lucky and Guinevere, assembled at that point the following morning. Lucky and Guinevere were horses, animals I had never taken a lot of notice of around our Salmon Arm shack, although I'd always thought it peculiar that they would let humans ride around on their backs.

George and Kathleen were not riding these horses, however. They walked and carried empty backpacks on their shoulders, and the horses wore strange-looking saddles composed of wooden frames whose ends crossed over at the top. To my surprise, Kathleen proceeded to heave the freight onto these frames, roping the sacks and boxes first on one side, then the other, until most of the freight was secured. All three humans stuffed their backpacks full, and the procession set off in single file along the narrow, rocky trail—George first, Kathleen second, then the two horses, followed by Chris and finally me. We wound our ponderous way through the forest, splashed across the small part of the river, clomped across the big wooden bridge, then took all the gear to the campsite. While the other humans and horses returned to their side of the river, Chris improved our shelter with tarps, built some crude pole shelves to hold her kitchen equipment and generally made life more comfortable for herself. I simply needed a dry place to curl up in—what a lot of work humans make for themselves just to deal with all their paraphernalia.

That night, while we huddled close to the stove to keep warm, Chris rummaged in one of the boxes and pulled out a small booklet that was illustrated with diagrams of trees with V-shaped bites taken out of them. Chris next lugged a heavy tool toward her, one of the very few items I ever saw her buy new, and mouthed words while glancing back and forth between the book and this machine. The tool in question was red and shiny, it smelled of oil and gas, and its business end was composed of a long snout well endowed with a multitude of vicious-looking teeth.

I found out its purpose the following morning. Chris took it the short distance upriver to the first site George and Kathleen had shown her. I could see that she was very apprehensive, which was unusual for her, and I kept looking round to see if there was a lurking danger I had somehow missed. Finally, with an expression of determination, she laid the little book on a fallen log and slid the padded cups she had used while driving the truck over her ears. She put the long-nosed tool on the ground, held it down with one foot, then took hold of a piece of rope and yanked furiously and repeatedly, to what purpose I could not at first imagine. After some time, Chris's face had turned almost the same shade as the tool. Then it suddenly spluttered and roared into life with such a hideous whine that I ran some distance away. The teeth on the long snout were whirling so swiftly, all I could see was a glittering blur. Chris took the tool to a nearby tree, gave the little book one more glance, took a deep breath, then plunged the whirling teeth into the tree's trunk.

She's going to kill it, I thought. And she did.

Within minutes, two great gouges had been made in the wood, and with a heartfelt sigh, the tree fell over and died. Chris didn't stop there; soon three or four more trees had succumbed, and the air was full of the scent of burned fuel and resin from the trees' terrible wounds. Next, Chris took an axe and started to lop off limbs, and finally she took up the red tool again, yanked the cord until it roared to life and butchered the trees into lengths. When she came back to camp that evening, she had a half-horrified, half-satisfied expression on her face.

After supper we walked over to George and Kathleen's house, where Chris picked up another jar of milk. "You should tie your dog up in camp while you're falling," said Kathleen. "It's too dangerous for her." Kathleen herself had killed a dog in just that way when she was young and building her own first cabin. I was grossly offended, not only at the prospect of being tied up, but also because Kathleen had used the phrase "your dog," as if Chris actually owned me. Chris unfortunately took this advice to heart, and for a day or two I had to suffer the indignity of being fastened with a collar and string. She soon let me loose, though, as she could see I had no intention of going anywhere near that hideous, murderous, ear-splitting machine.

As a result, my days throughout that summer stretched into one long round of boredom. My only delight was when Chris came back to the camp. Usually she would try to take me for a little hike at the end of the day, but she was so stressed out from the chainsaw and so achy from the heavy axe work that these hikes were only tokens. I couldn't understand why she was spending so much time doing all this, but humans, it seems, must always complicate their lives.

Readers of *Cabin at Singing River*, Chris's somewhat dispro-portionate account of our time at Lonesome Lake, will be largely familiar with the direction in which our lives developed from then on. In the book, Chris tells how she learned to fall and peel trees and how, with the help of the homesteaders and their horses, she dragged the logs to the bank of the river and eventually erected the large kennel into which she moved. (I say *she*, you notice—my indoor days were finished at the early puppy stage, and I was forced to find what shelter I could under the kennel's skimpy porch.)

Chris's version of these events, however, leaves much to be desired. During those four years, I was with her for almost every minute of every day, and what did I get? A few measly references to "the dog," without even the dignity of a name. Many readers of the book have asked Chris why this was the case; she always replied that it might have been too confusing to have both a Lonesome Lake and a Lonesome dog in the same manuscript. All I can say is that it shows Chris's supreme inadequacy as a writer. I feel very definitely that I should have been given better recognition for my services; hence my efforts with this memoir.

I WAS SOON able to match the different scents that surrounded us to the animals we met. Deer I was already familiar with; the large animal we had seen on the road, known by humans as moose, was present most of the time. As the summer progressed, the males' antlers developed into great wide platforms upon which both Tan Sister and I could have sat with ease. The moose we saw, however, were usually hornless females with young. We would often encoun-ter these ungainly creatures as we canoed along the river; if they met us on land, they ran swiftly away, but when we drifted by in the boat, they would stare at us curiously, as if our pact with the water monster merited some respect.

Deer mice, voles, lemmings, pocket gophers, shrews, pikas, marmots, squirrels, chipmunks—these represented the smaller, furry animals in our domain. Garter snakes slithered through the grass; little birds flittered in the trees, and larger ones hung over or floated on the water. Frogs and toads squatted along the shore, and bats squeaked over our heads at night. I was soon familiar with the mink; his tree-residing cousin, the marten; and his larger water relative, the otter. There were, I was relieved to note, no skunks. Canids were represented by foxes, coyotes and wolves—one time a pack of 10 had the temerity to howl right behind the house in broad daylight. I was so petrified, I would not come out from under the house for the rest of the day.

Despite this plethora of busy neighbours, however, my life was lacking something of great importance.

There was simply no one to play with.

Chris was never demonstrative in that way, and I could not at first believe that other human companionship was to be so lacking in my life. We were friendly with the homesteaders across the river, but our visits there were brief and businesslike. We went over almost every day; Chris fetched milk and took her vegetable scraps to the chickens, and she asked for logging and building advice when she needed it. That typical human social event, a nice companionable chat over a cup of coffee, never took place.

Not that Chris didn't talk—far from it. She gabbed all the time. She gabbed to the trees she was about to butcher, to the chainsaw (usually an imprecation of some sort, I'm afraid to say) and, most commonly, to herself. Occasionally she spared a passing word for me. It took me a while to get used to this paucity of conversation.

I well remember an incident that occurred a few days after we first arrived. It was late in the day, and Chris was huddled close to the stove, upon which she was cooking her supper. All of a sudden she laughed out loud and followed it with: "Well I'll be darned!" I was snoozing, and I leapt up with alacrity. Such happy oratory could only be directed at another person. To my bemusement, however, neither my nose nor my ears had registered anyone's arrival. Rapidly I looked in all directions for this other being.

But now Chris was laughing again—this time, as you might have guessed, at me. "Oh, Lonesome," she said. "I'm not talking to anyone. Look. I was reading this book. Something struck me funny, that's all. There's no one else here. You're going to have to get used to me talking to myself, you know."

I understood her words, for I was quite familiar with humanspeak by then, but still could not give up the idea that someone was about, and I continued to look for the person for some time. Believe it or not, Chris had the insensitivity to capitalize on my naïveté. Later, when she became famous, one of the standard questions people asked her was: "Don't you ever get lonely living way out there?" To which she would reply: "No, but my dog does!" Everyone would laugh and turn toward me with their mocking, gaping mouths. And yet nothing could have been closer to the truth.

CHRIS CHAINSAWED AND chopped and brush-piled and peeled for a while without a break. But when the moon had shrunk, then swollen and begun to wither again, she stuffed her sleeping bag and a sketchy camp into her pack, and off we went back along the trail down the river. At first I treated this expedition with apprehension, especially as I had to make my second crossing of Hunlen Creek, but the water had dropped considerably, and it was now a simple matter to leap across on the boulders. The closer to the road we got, the more excited I became. I even welcomed the sight of that hideous belching monster, the truck, hoping beyond hope that its appearance meant what I thought it did. Sure enough, after the agonized lurching over the tote road and past the lonely clearing where I was born, we finally reached the highway and eventually Tan Sister's house at Stuie.

My joy at seeing my littermate again knew no bounds (although protocol demanded that she go through the same tiresome barking, stiff-legged routine as when we first met). I knew that Chris had left her possessions behind in the bush, so it did not look as though we were going to stay outside for very long, but I vowed to live for the moment and not think too much about our return. And, indeed, we were at Stuie for only a day or two before we headed back into the bush; however, this was the start of a pattern that would persist for most of our time at Lonesome Lake—a once-a-month trip out to Stuie so that Chris could go on to Bella Coola for mail and a few odd items from the stores. I looked forward to these expeditions with great delight.

Although we had camped overnight on our initial journey to the homestead, we could now do the whole trip in a day. The canoe on Lonesome Lake speeded up the first part considerably, and when Chris later acquired another canoe for the smaller lake (which was known as the Stillwater), this made the journey much easier. Then, in ideal conditions, we could make the hike out to the truck by lunchtime. This happened but rarely, however; during the early part of the summer, Hunlen Creek swelled to monstrous proportions, and it was always a battle of wits to find a way across. During freeze-up and breakup, when the lakes could not be used, the scrambles around the edges were always time-consuming. In winter, although the roadway of the ice made lake travel swift again, the trails were icy and the days too short to travel many miles. On top of which, the tote road was often no longer driveable at that time, and if there was no traffic on the final 12 miles of highway, the whole laborious distance to Stuie had to be walked. Consequently, more often than not, we spent a night somewhere along the way, occasionally two if conditions were really difficult.

On one of our early trips to Stuie, another visitor arrived there. He drove up in a small beat-up pickup with a tall wooden crate on the back. Tire chains hung from the side of this crate, and they clanked and thumped in sympathy with the truck's lurches as it wallowed along the root-bound driveway. This banging preceded the noise of the motor by some considerable time, being thereafter a constant and distinctive signature of the man himself.

This tall, skinny human unwound himself from the seat of the truck. He wore grime-encrusted jeans, a filthy padded vest and a frayed shirt of indeterminate colour from whose ragged cuffs his long, bony hands protruded. A bright yellow hard hat topped this ensemble, accentuating the man's leanness, but his most striking feature was a long, luxuriant bone-coloured beard whose furthest locks touched the belt buckle at his waist.

Tan Sister had shown great excitement the moment the chains' clanking noise could be heard. And the minute the pickup drew to a halt, she was bouncing around the driver's door in a display of delighted abandon that I had never seen her use.

"Hullo, puppity dog," said the man, at once stooping to pat her. He had a voice not unlike the water monster that had lived in an old hand pump in a neighbour's yard in Salmon Arm. To get the water, humans wagged the handle up and down several times, during which the monster's cobwebby wheezing and muttering grew louder and louder until suddenly it vomited forth The Wet. However, there was nothing frightening about this man's voice, and I found myself beside Tan Sister, quite anxious for him to acknowledge me as well.

—*Guess what!* Tan Sister panted as she wriggled her rear end rapturously. —*Do you know who this is?*

"Guess who this is," Debbie unconsciously parroted as she came out of the house. "Do you recognize her?"

At which the man gazed at me and reached out to touch me with a kindness that was palpable, and the feel of those long, thin fingers brought back memories with a rush. No doubt you have guessed already; it was, of course, the old man who had owned the shack where I was born. Like Chris, he smelled of truck fuel and woodsmoke, but beneath the scent of everyday living was the enticing and unforgettable potpourri of garbage, unwashed clothing and cats.

The man's human name was Simon. (As puppies, we simply knew him as "The Man," for as far as we knew, he was the only human being in the world.) He now lived, it turned out, at the head of the Stillwater, the first lake on our way home. I had noticed a strong human scent on the bit of trail between that lake and the tote road, and I now realized it had come from him. His property was on the far side of the water from the route we had taken, buried in trees and some distance from the lake, which is why Chris had been unaware of it. Chris did not possess the second canoe when we first met Simon, and when she found that he kept a motorboat on the Stillwater, she was more than willing to coordinate her return to Lonesome Lake with his.

So, after the shopping trip and a day spent scribbling letters, Chris and Simon drove up the rocky track to the end of the road, the one truck lurching behind the other. The three of us then walked in a line up the trail to the Stillwater.

"I built this trail," Simon proudly told Chris.

"I thought your father made it originally, when he started the first homestead in the valley," Chris screeched. (Simon, you may remember, was very deaf.)

"He did, but it was a much cruder trail then. I've improved it and maintained it for Tweedsmuir Park all these years. It's part of the trail up to the Hunlen Falls lookout now." He showed Chris his stash of tools: a shovel, a fork and a garden rake with which he had made Zen-like patterns on the section he had groomed on his way out. "See? There's a marten—and a fox." The neat footprints trotted along the newly raked soil. "At this time of year, before the tourists get busy, it's possible to see every animal that uses this trail."

When we came to the lake, we did not cross the footbridge as we had done before (a bridge, needless to say, that Simon had built; I was to learn that he had considerable prowess as an engineer), but continued along the eastern shore until we reached his boat.

Now *this* was more like it. A canoe was all very well, but one had to sit in it pretty carefully to avoid tipping over, and if the wind was wrong, Chris worked like a maniac to make progress. But with a couple of yanks of a cord, Simon fired the motor to life, and we putt-putted gently up the lake, against the remains of the current.

"This used to be a stretch of the river," Simon explained. "It was a very calm stretch; that's why the old trappers called it the Stillwater. But in the big rains of '37, Goat Creek went on the rampage and spilled that boulder fan across the valley right where the bridge is, so now we have a lake. I've been taking some of the boulders out of the river to try and drop the water level so it's not too deep in the creeks through my meadow for the fish when they want to lay their eggs."

Snags still peppered the drowned valley, and these were tenanted by tree swallows and flickers and other hole-nesting birds. Green cushions of water-monster hair undulated in the current as we entered the river channel and followed its winding course through the flat, marshy valley. The river began to get very shallow, even in this flooded time, but we squeezed between some willows and motored slowly up a narrow creek channel overhung with branches.

For some time I had been aware of the smell of cows; now a rangy bull glared at us from a small corral beneath the trees. "His lady friends are out grazing in the meadow," Simon wheezed. "I'm making a hay meadow from the bush. Come on, I'll show you round."

We docked the boat and jumped out into a patch of cedar forest, but a short walk brought us to a clearing where willow brush had been piled for burning and new grass was beginning to sprout between massive, blackened, upturned roots. "I've had to dig all these channels to drain the place," Simon explained, pointing to a neat ditch arrowing with great exactitude through the swampy ground. "And while I was working on this one, a grouse used this very log to drum on. He never minded me at all.

"And here," he indicated, "is the hay barn I'm building. I move the logs with this donkey engine. It's a pretty handy machine; all I need to do when I want to move it is tie its cable to a tree and let it winch its way to its new position."

Chris was impressed. She kept exclaiming and making admiring comments—always at triple the volume she would normally use (even when she was mad) to allow for Simon's deafness.

"This is fantastic soil, once it's drained," Simon grinned. We had come to the garden, which at this time of year was showing neat rows of young carrot and potato tops. Simon yanked at a couple of enormous rough-haired leaves and out popped the most gigantic radish I had ever seen. The swollen purple roots were as big as a human fist.

"But they're delicious!" Chris bellowed in amazement, having rubbed off the soil and taken a bite. "I'd have expected a radish of this size to be hollow or woody. But it's absolutely perfect." And she munched away blissfully as we continued our walk.

"There's not a rock in this soil," Simon was saying. "Clearing the land is really easy. The spruces and cedars have shallow roots that spread in a great big circle. All I do is take the chainsaw and cut right into the soil about 10 feet in a ring around the tree. Next big wind, and the tree falls right over all by itself."

Our tour brought us back a slightly different way, and it was apparent by the concentration of aromas that we were coming to the man's dwelling. Finally, a small plywood shack loomed through the network of trees, and I did a double take. Sure enough, squatting behind an enormous pile of empty plastic coffee-whitener jars was exactly the same building under which I had been born.

"I made it so it could be dismantled into components and easily transported," Simon explained proudly. "The Parks Board asked me to design a building that they could move around by helicopter."

But I was hardly listening, for as we approached the door, my attention was instantly taken by a sudden scuffle from within the building. As the door swung open, there was an absolute eruption of cats. Some flew through the door; some leapt for the roof; some streaked into the trees; some dived beneath the floor.

"Wow," Chris laughed. "How many have you got?"

"'Bout 18 at last count," Simon wheezed. Judging by the smell that billowed out in the felines' wake, I would have said that 18 was a pretty conservative estimate.

The cats were not the only source of the impressive effluvium that now assailed our nostrils. I could see by the slight narrowing of her eyes and the sudden opening of her mouth that even Chris was aware of it. Now, housekeeping is definitely not one of Chris's strong attributes, but the inside of Simon's shack was like no other human dwelling I have ever smelled. Every available space was jammed with piles of old books and mouldering magazines that had long ago been welded together with damp. Chips spilled from a straggling woodpile; some cats had used this area as a bathroom, and the stench was amazing. A stepladder gave access to a hole in the ceiling (from which several pairs of glittering eyes observed us); this, apparently, was where Simon slept.

Buried among the junk was the old, familiar Coleman gas stove. Simon waved a kettle. "Coffee?" he asked.

I could see Chris hesitating, but "Sure," she yelled determinedly and smiled. Simon unearthed a wobbly kitchen chair from beneath a cascade of magazines, and Chris perched herself upon it, sitting as close as possible to the open door. While the water boiled, Simon rummaged around on the floor, bringing to light two cracked mugs. "Pointless hanging them up," he explained. "Cats just knock 'em down again." He tipped scalding water into both of them, swirled them with a practised air, tossed the liquid out the door, sniffed the mugs cautiously (very much like a cat), then spooned instant coffee into the mugs and refilled them.

"Coffee-mate?" Simon asked.

Chris shook her head. "Cheers," she said bravely and knocked it back.

∾

AFTER THAT, WHEN bad weather or short days made travel upriver too difficult, we often spent the night at Simon's place. He

As the door swung open, there was an absolute eruption of cats.

loved to give us a tour of the property. He'd dug a whole network of ditches to drain his swampy hay meadows, but he was equally proud of the spawning channels he had thus created, and in the spring he would show us the baby fish that flitted about in the warm, shallow water. Simon had no horses to clear his land, as George and Kathleen did, but used instead the heavy, squat, oily machine from which a veritable spider's web of steel cables issued. Simon had referred to it as a donkey engine, although as far as I could see there was no resemblance between it and a donkey whatsoever.

Simon always had dozens of stories of his encounters with bear and moose and deer, and he told us how the former would always stare at him, unafraid, and the latter would take food from his hands. He spoke of the seven different-coloured violets that he'd found on his property, the ivory-billed woodpeckers he had seen (Chris told me later they were supposed to be extinct) and the Sasquatch tracks he had observed one winter on his way to Bella Coola.

Before we had our own canoe on the Stillwater, Simon would ferry us back over the river so we could connect with the trail up to Lonesome Lake. On one of these occasions, I noticed that Simon had picked up a tool. It was long and thin, vaguely reminiscent of a whisk broom in shape, but its wider end was solid. I had seen—and smelled—these objects several times in people's houses. The home-steaders had a couple, and even Chris had one. But I had never seen them used and had no idea as to their purpose.

So when we reached the open space beside the river, and Simon muttered something about "checking the sights" (I assumed he was talking about the view), I had not the faintest notion of what was about to happen. Simon lodged the wider part of the broom-like thing against his shoulder and pointed the other end toward the far mountain. Without warning, my brain seemed to implode. The shock was immense. My wits fled to the four winds. I shook my head to try and get rid of the awful ringing that persisted in my ears.

As my senses slowly returned, I became aware of a strong, acrid scent in the air. It was a scent I would never forget. From that moment, this aroma began to weave an insidious thread through my life. And as my experience with it grew, I would come to associate it with something far more ominous than the shock and the noise. For it became, in my mind, inexorably linked with death.

But despite this terrible experience, insensitivity toward animals was rare on Simon's part, and, like Tan Sister, I found the man easy to love. Particularly so because we had something in common. Like me, Simon was lonely.

During the summer, when he worked on the trail or drove back and forth along the tote road, he often met hikers who were going to Hunlen Falls. He took some of these people home with him and gave them a tour of his estate.

One day, during the second summer that Chris and I lived in the area, we could see that a change had occurred on the property. In front of the shack was a network of string, poles and flagging tape that glittered in the dappled heat of the August sun. There was a sharp smell of newly cut cedar and a raw pile of sawdust nearby.

"I'm going to build an extension," said Simon proudly. "I've started cutting some of the lumber with an Alaskan Mill."

"That's marvellous," Chris shouted. "It's going to be quite a size." A new batch of kittens was tumbling on the floor of the shack, and she picked one up and began to tickle its stomach.

"This here's going to be the living room," Simon explained, pointing to a rectangle of string, "and this a bedroom, and this the bathroom." For someone who didn't even have an outhouse, this was going to be quite a leap.

"It's time you extended your living area," Chris agreed at full volume.

"It's probable," said Simon carefully, busying himself with the coffee routine, "that someone else is going to come and live here."

"That's wonderful," Chris shouted, astonished. "Is it anybody I know?"

Simon rummaged on the floor for the mugs.

"It's somebody I met," he said. "A hiker." He handed Chris a steaming mug. They drank in silence for a moment.

"I've got a picture of her," he blurted, suddenly nervous, scrubbing at the dirt-ingrained creases on his neck. People often sent him snapshots after they had visited his place, but instead of producing one of these, Simon reached into the clutter beside his chair and pulled out the latest catalogue from Sears.

"She's a model," he said dreamily, holding the book between fingers that trembled slightly. "She hiked up here with some friends." He spread his hands apart and the book flopped open. "It's funny, but it always opens at that page, all by itself."

The section in the catalogue displayed items in the furniture department. The page portrayed a glossy couch, beside which was a glossy table, and upon which sat a glossy woman, smiling a glossy smile. The woman was about the same age as Chris, but a lot slimmer. She appeared to be talking brightly into the telephone; I wondered who she was speaking to. Was she sending messages to Simon that none of the rest of us could hear?

Chris, for once, was struck dumb. She carefully put her empty coffee mug onto the cold heater stove.

"Do you know when she's coming?" she said at last.

"Probably later in the summer," said Simon in a rush. "She said I'd got a fantastic place. She said she'd love to live here."

Chris stared in sorrow at the back of the old man's bowed head. "I'm sure she did," she said gently (or at least as gently as it is possible to be when you are bellowing at full decibels). "You have indeed got an amazing place here." She pushed herself to her feet. "Well, I guess we ought to be going. We've got to get through the bad bear patch before it gets too dark."

"Well, Lonesome," she said to me later as we hiked through the forest. "I wonder what's going to come of this?"

It was several months before we again set foot on Simon's place. We had completed a mail run and were heading back upriver to Chris's big kennel (which was, by that time, almost complete). The days had shortened and the fall rains were in full spate. By the time we reached the Stillwater, the weather had deteriorated into a wild storm that drove the first sleety snow of winter in great spirally swirls between the thrashing trees. The only sheltered area for camping would be in the section of forest between the two lakes, which was thick with hungry, pre-hibernation bears. If we continued to Lonesome Lake, where it was safer to camp, we would be at the mercy of that terrible wind. So, having scrambled exhaustedly around the Stillwater, Chris waded the river (only knee deep for her right then, but a considerably unpleasant exercise for me) and headed for Simon's shack. Even within the gloom of the forest, the wind tugged and battered, and snowflakes whirled between the branches, winking briefly like fireflies before they melted on the sodden forest floor.

The little shack sported its familiar comforting plume of smoke and overpowering stench. Little seemed to have changed since our last visit in the summer. In front of the shack sprawled the network of poles and string; some of the flagging tape still jiggled at the corners, but most of it was faded and torn. The pile of sawdust from the Alaskan Mill had greyed in the rains, and the tarp that had covered the new-sawn boards had long since been frayed into tatters by the wind.

Simon, as always, was pleased to have us visit, and he happily told us about the mama bear who had sat on her bottom and cuddled her two cubs in her lap to nurse them just like human babies, and the cougar who spent the night in his hay barn and stared at him unafraid, and the fish that came to his line when he whistled for them in a certain way. Of the dream home and its erstwhile resident there was no mention.

After a supper of canned stew enriched with Coffee-mate, Chris relinquished her hard kitchen chair and retired to bed. There was a wall-less shed, originally built as a hay barn but now full of rotting junk, near the shack, and Chris elected to place her bedroll between boxes and under a bit of plastic rather than fight the cats for space on the warmer, drier, litter-box floor. As she manoeuvred some of the packages by flashlight, a Sears catalogue slipped onto the ground. Chris turned the flashlight beam upon it—it had fallen open at the furniture-department page, all by itself. At its edges, the book was sodden and softened with rain, but the smooth centre of the page portrayed a glossy woman on a glossy couch, smiling into the telephone her perennially glossy smile.

With whom, I wondered, was she communicating now?

CHAPTER SEVEN

AMONG THE PECULIARITIES THAT SET Chris apart from most of the other people we knew was her habit of making marks on pieces of paper. Some of these were executed with a tool like the end of a squirrel's tail; with this she slopped colour onto the surface, creating what she referred to as paintings. They seemed to have no use other than to cover the drafty places in the walls, but her fellow humans seemed to like them so much they were even prepared to trade money for them. And money was something Chris was always on the lookout for. About once a year, she would roll the paintings into an unused length of stovepipe and backpack or toboggan them to the road. We would then travel to some town or other, sometimes all the way back to Salmon Arm, and have an art show. Although the setting-up process plunged Chris into her usual foul temper, once everything was in order she wallowed in the praise that was afforded her. She obviously enjoyed that part of the show as much as the money, and it was quite degrading to see her lap it all up. Before coming home there would be an orgy of shopping for tools, food and bags of kibble, and back into the mountains we would go.

The paintings were not produced until after she had moved into the cabin, which was during our second fall at Lonesome Lake. But long before that, indeed for all the time I had known her, she had made other kinds of marks on paper with a special stick that bled blue sap. The marks looked like chicken scratches and were incomprehensible to me for a long time, but then Chris unearthed a couple of boxes that had so far remained unopened and extracted yet another tool. Really, humans' possessions are of an infinite and puzzling variety. The tool was housed in its own square box with a lid, and when the lid was removed, intricate slivers of metal vaguely reminiscent of rib bones were revealed. Chris fed a piece of paper into the back of the machine and pressed one of the many buttons that ranged along the front. At once, one of the ribs flew up. It had a little hammer on its end, and it put yet another kind of mark on the pristine white surface of the paper. Each button created a different shape, and soon the little hammers were pattering in fine style, leaving a line of tidy footprints. When the edge of the paper was reached, there was a loud *ding!* Chris swiped at a lever, the paper and its housing crashed to the left, and soon another line of footprints emerged.

Chris would often do this activity while sitting on the porch, so I had plenty of opportunity to observe it in detail. As her fingers hit the buttons, she always spoke aloud, but much more slowly than usual, often breaking the words up into their component parts. It wasn't long before I understood that the little shapes corresponded to sounds, and when the sounds were clumped together, like a string of toad's eggs, they made human words. I also learned that the tool was called a typewriter.

Chris had always written long chicken-scratch letters to her mother and friends, but a year or so after we had moved into the cabin, her writing grew more intense. Instead of accepting the first draft, she would often screw up the paper and use it the next time she needed to light the stove. With her brows drawn into a frown, she would attempt to rearrange the words into what she felt might be a better order. As we walked through the forest, she would mutter to herself, then often scribble into a little notebook; these musings would be transferred onto the clean white paper in the typewriter after we arrived home.

On one of our trips to Bella Coola, Chris carried an extra letter to the post office, one that had been typed and retyped and read aloud a number of times. It contained a fairly uninteresting account of her cabin-building efforts and a bit about the journey to the road. She never mentioned me at all. This letter was mailed with the others, and I noted a slightly apprehensive look on Chris's face as she pushed the letter into the slot. As usual, it was another moon before we returned to town—and the whole of Bella Coola was talking about this letter. Unbeknown to me—and everyone else for that matter, for she had not breathed a word to a soul—the letter had been sent to a radio station, to Peter Gzowski's *Morningside* on the CBC, and had been read on the air. It had been broadcast clean across the country—even, Tan Sister told me, as far away as Ontario.

Chris, I am afraid to say, was insufferable. She basked in this praise like a queen. She had been given the producer's phone number, and when she called they told her they would love to have more. As a consequence, for the next couple of years Chris carried another of these letters with her whenever we went out to the post office. She had always maintained she didn't need other humans to talk to, but here she was, unburdening her soul to literally millions of people. I listened while Chris composed every one, and in all that time, with one single exception that I shall deal with later in this narrative, I was never alluded to.

Interestingly enough, we could not receive the radio signal at Lonesome Lake, so we never heard the letters broadcast, but that didn't stop Chris from sending them. She might have professed to have a solitary nature, but she could not deny that she loved all the attention that the letters gave her.

CHAPTER EIGHT

"IT'S SUCH A PRIVILEGE," CHRIS would often state to whomever was within reach of her endlessly expressed opinions (usually only me), "to live in a country where animals like bears still exist." Privilege, my paw! My idea of privilege would be to have a safe house, a warm bed, predictable meals, walks in a well-used park, bridges crossing all the rivers, a vehicle that purred quietly and ran smoothly instead of battering my eardrums and bruising my poor body with every lurch, lots of congenial company and a few treats once in a while.

But what I got was a hole I had to dig myself under the floor of the huge log kennel that Chris eventually built, a hole that was only partially protected from the weather and provided even less of a barrier against the flies.

And what I also got was bears. At least they slept for part of the year, but they were a constant threat from the moment the dandelions thrust rosettes of leaves into the clearing beside the cabin until long after the first snow covered the ground. At Stuie, I felt comparatively safe, for Tan Sister was quite aggressive toward them, and the two of us would have high old times barking like lunatics and chasing them up trees. Bears were the only thing I ever did bark at; whenever I smelled that rank, musty smell, something came over me and I just could not help myself. It was a funny thing, though, that when I met a bear alone, without Tan Sister beside me, although I would bark just as loudly and confidently, the bears never took the slightest bit of notice. These encounters always ended with me beating an ignominious retreat beneath the house.

One of the reasons the bears were so prevalent in that place was an annual phenomenon peculiar only to the coastal areas of western North America. Every year when the birch leaves paled and began to fall, the sockeye salmon swam upriver to spawn. One morning the gravel bed shifting under the silvery coils of the water monster would be empty of any visible creature; the next, wavering ruby flags would be slithering like weeds in the current. Within a week, the river would be full of leaping, swimming, slopping, swaying fish.

At first the splatter and slither excited me. I thought these animals were having a wonderful game, and I was only too delighted to try and join them. But I rapidly discovered that they were merely extensions of The Wet; what is more, they tried to bring that unpleasant substance to me by flapping their tails and bashing it into my eyes. I didn't think this fair at all; having the water monster on their side made their games far too rough. I soon tired of them and left them alone.

Chris, for some reason, was mightily intrigued by this annual piece of theatre. She spent many hours staring into the water and watching the sinuous movements, exclaiming at the colours and patterns that the antics of the fish produced. I, however, soon found that the advent of these animals had a result that was far from entertaining. It was, in fact, downright dangerous. Once they had procreated, the salmon died, and the strong smell, while not unpleasing in itself, had very dire consequences. For an aromatic, rotting fish is a gourmet morsel of incomparable delight for a bear.

Now, I have never enjoyed eating the fish in their slimy stage.

The Wet, at that point, is still too much part of their makeup. But once the carcasses have dried, I love to crunch them up. When you see in pet-food stores such weird concoctions as sanitized pigs' ears (which, like most processed foods, have neither flavour nor nutritional value), it's a wonder people haven't cottoned on to desiccated fish carcasses as a doggy treat. The patentees of such a delectable delicacy would make a fortune, I assure you. But when the fish are still limp and slimy? Ugh! Only a creature as depraved as a bear could ever get excited about one of those.

Despite Chris's odd attitudes toward bears, she did have enough brains to treat them with a great deal of respect. The first time the bears began to congregate for the salmon, the kennel was far from completed, being nothing more than a walled enclosure. (Why on earth she had to build such a big one, I can't begin to imagine.) Even Chris realized that a tent was hardly the best dwelling under these circumstances, especially as it was situated right on the banks of the river, and she moved camp into one of George and Kathleen's storage sheds for the duration of the fall. When increasingly poor weather made even this shelter too uncomfortable, we hiked out to Tan Sister's place, where we spent the rest of the winter. (Tan Sister wasn't there. She and her pack had made the long journey back to that far-off country, Ontario.)

Although she spent almost every waking hour of the following spring, summer and fall involved with that kennel, Chris seemed to take an inordinately long time to accomplish anything; when the second spawning season came around, the building was still unfinished. It had no floor, no door, no windows in the window holes and only half a roof; nevertheless, the day the first fish began to colonize the gravel bars, she moved our camp and all its bits and pieces onto a few planks laid across the floor joists in one of the dry corners. I dug a little bed for myself in a pile of sawdust in the other. The building was finally finished at a point during that winter, and in subsequent years Chris would take great delight in telling people that she could sit on the porch of her cabin and watch grizzlies feeding in the river not more than a stone's throw away.

But I, who was once more banished to the outside and had only the confines of the hole beneath the floor for protection, was often terrified out of my wits. If Chris was sitting beside me, I didn't feel so bad. But once she had gone to bed and left me on my own, I barked.

—*Keep away*, I would yell. —*This is my territory. Keep away.*

"Shut up, Lonesome!" Chris would roar.

—*I'm really a wolf who is 10 feet tall. I can beat you all up with one paw tied behind my back. Keep away. Keep away. Keep away. Keep away.*

"For God's sake, SHUT UP," Chris would scream.

But it was as if another being had taken hold of me. I simply couldn't stop.

One night, the bears were more numerous than they had ever been before. Mothers snarled at growling cubs; fathers roared and grunted. My barking became incessant—and so did Chris's shouting. I've never liked anyone speaking sharply to me; I've always had sensitive ears, and now I'd had enough.

Right, I thought, if that's the way she wants it, I'm off. Only a maniac would want to come and live in a place like this in any case. I'm getting out of here.

And I set off down the river, alone.

It was the most frightening experience of my life. I'm not really sure why I thought that travelling down the river, in the dark, in bear country, would improve my lot, but once started I was too terrified to return. There were bears everywhere, particularly in the stretch of forest between the two lakes. My nose told me of their proximity most of the time, and I avoided them as best I could, but a nose is only as good as the prevailing breeze. Sometimes I inadvertently got too close to them and was startled by a chop of teeth and a crunch of brittle fishbone or, on one occasion, a slavering growl. In these instances I was saved only by the nimbleness of my feet. Fortunately, the bears were not really interested in me; they were concentrating on eating and could see little point in expending energy by chasing an active animal while surrounded by so much (ugh!) food.

It had been quite late when I set off, and light was already beginning to steal into the sky when I reached the Stillwater. By this time, I was so exhausted by terror that when a whiff of Simon's establishment socked me in the nose, I could think of one thing only—the safe haven that he represented.

But to get there, I had to cross The Wet.

The river, at that point, had widened to a broad sweep as a prelude to entering the lake. At that time of year it was fairly shallow—the deepest part would not have covered Chris's knees—but for me it was a formidable barrier. However, the thought of the hot ursine breath and dripping fangs hovering behind me was so disturbing that I deemed the water monster the lesser of the two evils and plunged right in. I arrived at Simon's shack dripping wet.

"Hullo, puppity dog," said the old man, surprised. He bent to fondle my ears with his deliciously sensitive fingers. "What are you doing here so early? Why, you're soaking wet."

—*The bears*, I panted. —*Shout—grizzlies—fish* . . . I was no longer coherent in my anguish.

Simon straightened up, puzzled, and looked around. "And where," he said, beginning to sound concerned, "is Chris?"

"SHE'S SUCH A faithful little dog," said Michael worriedly.

"I know," Simon agreed. "She's never parted from Chris for a moment."

"Isn't Chris due out tomorrow?" said Debbie, consulting the calendar. "Yes, she is. How long did you wait after Lonesome arrived?"

"A couple of hours," Simon wheezed. "What bothered me was the condition Lonesome was in when she showed up. She was soaking wet, and you know what a funny little thing she is about water. The current can be quite tricky where Lonesome Lake empties into the river. A canoe did get swept into the river once. It was smashed to bits in the rapids. Chris might have made a mistake while beaching the canoe."

"Did you walk up to Lonesome Lake to see if there was any sign of her there?" said Michael.

"I did, and saw nothing. But if she'd misjudged the current, there wouldn't be any sign from the trail anyway."

"And no sign of any struggle with bears, or abandoned gear?" said Debbie.

"No."

"I suppose," said Michael thoughtfully, "the thing to do is to find out when or even if she left the homestead. If the days were longer, she wouldn't have set off until tomorrow morning, but at this time of year she would probably have started today. What time did Lonesome get to your place?"

"Not long after sunrise," said Simon. "Chris would never

have reached my place at that time if she'd left this morning."

"How can we find out for sure whether she left?" Debbie asked. "We can't phone the homestead and ask them."

"I guess we'll have to inform the RCMP," said Michael slowly. "They must have some kind of rescue organization in place. I suppose they'll have to fly to Lonesome Lake, then walk up to the homestead. That would be the quickest way to find out if Chris left at all."

"But it will still take several hours," Debbie pointed out. "Poor Lonesome. Look at her. She knows there's something dreadfully wrong. Look at the anxious expression on her face. She's quite distraught."

At which a considerable amount of consoling and patting ensued, but as you might imagine, my agitation was for very different reasons than these poor misguided humans had supposed.

—*Chris is perfectly okay*, I tried to tell them. —*She's simply become too hard to live with anymore. Haven't you ever heard of Doggylib? The way she was treating me is no longer politically correct. I have a perfect right not to put up with it.*

But no matter how much I tried to explain, none of them grasped an inkling of the truth.

It was all Chris's fault, I reasoned with myself: a) she shouldn't have shouted at me, and b) she should have given me better protection against the bears. But at the bottom of it all was a niggling worm of conscience that kept my head hung and ears drooping. "She's such a faithful little dog" had been Michael's first words upon our arrival at Stuie; words that summed up the code by which I had always tried to live. And for the first time in my life, I had broken it.

—*She shouldn't have shouted at me so*, I wailed hopelessly to

Tan Sister when all my efforts to get through to the humans had failed. At which Tan Sister merely shrugged.

—*You've been around long enough to learn how to stand up for yourself,* she intimated with a twitch of her eyebrow. —*What is it now? Four years that you've had that human? You've either got to take her as she is or abandon her. Thin-skinned sensitivity isn't going to get you very far in this world.* And she trotted over to the bank and peered proprietarily at the meadow, her nose tuned nonchalantly toward the river (the strong aromas left me in no doubt that a well-used spawning ground with attendant banqueting bears existed here, too), displaying a control over her environment that I could never hope to emulate.

CHRIS'S STORY, NEEDLESS to say, came out when she met up with Debbie and Michael and Simon.

"When I woke up," she said, "Lonesome had gone. She's such a faithful little dog!" (How I cringed when I heard that!) "And such a wimp, too." (That was somewhat less flattering.) "I never dreamed that she would go off all by herself. I figured her barking had infuriated a bear and she had run off in terror and got eaten." So instead of setting out and getting to Simon's that morning as she had intended to do, Chris had started a search. While Simon was walking up and down the river below Lonesome Lake looking for Chris's canoe or her remains, she was similarly employed, at the top end, looking for me. She called and called, examined tracks, checked all the log-jams up and down the river, but, of course, to no avail.

Although she knew she might be a little late meeting Simon, she figured that the date of her intended arrival at Stuie was the important one to keep. She always told her friends when she was expected out, and she didn't want ever to be overdue as that, she was well aware, might create unnecessary worry. Although the days were short and the bear danger high, she figured that if she really pushed it, she could still make it to the road in one day. She had, of course, no idea of what was going on downstream.

She made good time down Lonesome Lake, strode happily between the rivers, scrambled around the Stillwater and hiked rapidly over the trail to the truck. At one point in the journey, while she was in the forested stretch between the two lakes, she heard a plane flying low overhead, apparently following the river. But Chris thought nothing of it; at that time of year, Fisheries liked to count the spawning salmon, and she assumed the plane had been hired to transport personnel. She could barely see the plane through the canopy of the forest, and, perforce, the occupants of the aircraft could not see her. She had absolutely no idea that the passengers in the aircraft were RCMP officers looking for her.

She had reached the truck and driven most of the way along the boulder-strewn tote road to the highway when Simon's pickup lurched slowly to meet her. In the wooden crate with its flapping chains were Debbie, Michael—and me. I had heard Chris's truck before the others were aware of it, and I began to anticipate something of the nature of our meeting. I put on my most woeful expression of contrition and jammed my tail far between my legs. Chris, I figured, was going to be plenty mad.

But, "Lonesome!" Chris exclaimed, her features a mixture of astonishment and delight. "I thought you were eaten by a bear!" And I'll be doggoned if she didn't give me a hug.

"Actually," muttered Michael dryly, and with no little embarrassment, "we figured the same about you."

It took Chris a little while to cotton on. "You mean, you thought . . . ? The police . . . And the plane was looking for me? But I'm not overdue. I'm out on the day I said I would be. Why . . . ?"

"We thought you might have got the date wrong," Debbie supplied. "You've done that before—you remember that time you came out two days early? And when Lonesome arrived at Simon's all wet, he thought . . . and we thought . . ." and out the story came.

"I don't believe this," said Chris, turning to me in utter astonishment. "Lonesome, you—you rat." Well, if being called a rat (of all things!) was all the punishment I was going to get, I guessed I could put up with that. I looked suitably sorry; humans are actually pretty easy to manipulate with a little bit of body language. Michael had already heard from the RCMP that they had reached the homestead and found out Chris had left that morning, sans me, upon which they had all driven up the tote road to meet her. Once it was all sorted out, the whole thing seemed to die down very quickly without any fuss.

But I still possessed that niggling worm of guilt for deserting Chris so precipitously. I knew that this would undermine the absolute trust Chris had in my loyalty. I wondered what I could do to rectify the situation. That evening, Tan Sister came up with a scheme that was bound to ensure my complete forgiveness.

—*You really think it will work?* I asked.

—*Guarantee it,* Tan Sister stated firmly.

And so, when Chris prepared to drive downvalley to Bella Coola the following day, I jumped into the back of the truck and refused to get out.

"Come on, Lonesome. I'm only going shopping. You'll be bored to death in there all day." She grabbed my front feet and hauled me over the tailgate. At which I promptly jumped in again.

"Oh, for goodness' sake," Chris grumbled. "Be it on your own head, then. At least it isn't raining." But I could see, as Tan Sister had predicted, that she was secretly pleased at my obvious demonstration of faithfulness, and away we drove together.

As usual, Chris parked the truck not far from the Co-op and started to walk around the three stores. It wasn't long before she encountered someone she knew and started to talk. She might never have needed to buy much in town, but a shopping expedition was full of friendly meetings and invariably took all day.

Bella Coola is populated with numerous dogs, many of whom stroll in gossiping phalanxes, sniff at the many messages left by their fellows (which is called, in modern parlance, checking out one's pee-mail) or sit in idle groups enjoying the sun. They often hang out by the Co-op doors, which are those automatic sliding ones; if you stand in front of them, an invisible eye sees you and causes the doors to open all by themselves. Many of the town dogs have learned how to operate the invisible eye. When it's cold, they stand on the magic spot and cause the doors to whoosh open while they bask in the warm air billowing out.

As I am such a polite and retiring individual, I usually receive little more than a cursory acknowledgment from those strangers who are well bred enough to know their manners, and for the most part I stay in the truck where I am supposed to be. But for some reason on this particular morning, I received an unprecedented amount of attention from the other canine inhabitants of the town. I assumed, at first, that the account of our adventures had already hit the sidewalks (which news invariably does with amazing rapidity in Bella Coola), and heady with the euphoria of fame,

I forgot myself entirely, and out of the truck I jumped.

Chris still had her back to me. But the person to whom she was talking did not.

"Is your dog in heat?" the other woman said.

"No," I heard Chris scoff.

"Well, she's sure acting like it," said Chris's friend.

Chris whirled around.

But I was already involved in a situation from which it had become impossible to extricate myself.

The animal who had so firmly engaged my attention was black and long-coated like me, but with a softer sweep to his fur that looked more in the style of a setter. He had an elegance of manner and a strong desire to please; a more perfect gentleman one could not wish to meet. Although our time together was lamentably short, I can truthfully say that we became remarkably attached to each other.

Chris's brows drew down into a V of fury. Had we been alone, I could well imagine the rage that would have ensued. But in the presence of other people she was forced to control herself. There was little she could do about it by then anyway.

I spent the rest of my day shut inside the cab.

❧

"HOW LONG IS it for a dog?" I heard Chris say to the homesteaders some time after we had arrived home. Rains had washed much of the stench of rotting fish away, the leaves had shrivelled on the alders, the last bears were plodding up the game trail behind the cabin on the way to their winter hangouts, and the first flakes of snow had begun to fall.

"Five months, I think," was the reply.

"She doesn't seem to be showing much yet. Perhaps it won't happen."

But as the winter solstice passed and the snow began to accumulate in earnest, it became obvious that changes to my physiology were taking place. To begin with, the hole through which I squeezed to get to my nest under the porch had become puzzlingly tight; then I began to have difficulty lying comfortably, especially when I tried to curl into a ball. I became tired and sluggish and short of wind; the skin on my belly began to feel strained and stretched. One day Chris set off on a monstrous hike up a nearby mountain on snowshoes, and as the snow grew deeper at higher altitudes, I found it extraordinarily difficult to keep up.

"You can go home if you want," Chris said, not unkindly, as she paused to look at me with a certain amount of concern. But obedience and duty were still a very strong part of my makeup, particularly after the recent lamentable lapses, and when Chris finally rested upon the summit, she was considerably surprised to find that I was still gasping slowly up behind.

"Poor little Lonesome," she said, remarkably solicitous for once. "It's not much fun being female sometimes, is it?"

During that February, Michael, Debbie, their little boy (who actually was not that little anymore) and Tan Sister wanted to go away for a while, and they asked Chris if we would look after their house, mainly to stoke the fires so the waterbed wouldn't freeze. So we took leave of the homesteaders, skied down the frozen lakes and picked our way over the icy trails to Stuie.

Every day, no matter where we were, Chris liked to go for a hike. In winter, at Stuie, when the outlying channels are frozen, it is possible to get right out onto the wide gravel flats that surround the Talchako River. This body of water joins our river a short distance below Stuie, whence they form a single stream that eventually slides into the sea.

The Talchako is fed from an immense icefield, and it is a much colder river than ours. In winter it is always much choked with whorls and ridges and plates of piled, greenish ice. Black snakes and bubbles of water roil through this bitter landscape. In my less energetic state, I soon discovered that walking on the river ice was far easier than slogging through the softer snow that lay on the gravel bars. Chris kept trying to make me walk in her footsteps, but the ease of the ice was too tempting.

I thought I was keeping well away from the water monster, but his perfidy knows no bounds. The solidity of the ice was but an illusion; there was a crack, a frigid breath from below, and through the ice I went.

"Oh no!" Chris gasped, running toward me as fast as the soft snow would allow. (It always astonishes me how verbal humans are in distress—some dogs, too. When faced with a disaster, I much prefer to reserve my energies for whatever other physical activities are required.)

Normally, I am sure, I could have pulled myself out unaided. But my enormously swollen belly got in the way. I got my front feet onto an ice shelf, but my back paws flailed uselessly in the water. I kept my eyes on Chris in mute appeal.

She, however, did not rush up to me right away. She stopped on the bank and looked worriedly at the ice. The river flats were littered with logs and jams, and at that point, an ancient tree trunk was thrust like a finger into the water; it was, indeed, the swirl of the current around the end of this log that had given the water monster the excuse to form such a treacherous surface.

Chris straddled the log (which was encrusted with snow) and

inched her way along it on her belly. At the furthest point at which she felt able to go, she could just reach my middle left toe. She grasped it—it hurt. She pulled; I scrabbled. And with my poor swollen belly scraping along the edge of the ice, I popped out like a dipper onto an ice floe.

Having been immersed for some little while, and having never had a very good under-fur, I was, needless to say, quite soaked. I at once shook myself hard. But it was minus 30 degrees Fahrenheit that day (I heard Chris say later), and the wind was howling down the river flats something cruel. The instant I shook my fur, the water turned to ice.

"Come, Lonesome. Quick," said Chris. And she began to lope as quickly as possible back toward the house. I had to struggle hard to keep up with her. We had quite a way to go, but once off the flats we entered the forest, so at least the wind was somewhat lessened; my coat, however, jangled like a set of wind chimes and provided an interesting counterpoint to the squeal of the snow underfoot.

To my enormous surprise—and gratification—Chris opened the door of the house and ushered me inside. She found an old foamy and got me to lie down on it beside the fire. This was an unprecedented luxury indeed. For once in my life I was able to stretch languidly in unaccustomed warmth; I was even able to ignore the raw scrapes on my belly.

After a while, however, I began to feel a little unwell. Unwarranted pressures and turbulences began to pervade my abdomen, and sometimes little pains would flicker through. This condition worsened over the next two days, and I could see that Chris was starting to become concerned. And indeed, I made no attempt to hide my own worry and discomfort, for I began to feel very peculiar indeed.

Suddenly, I was racked with a pain of great magnitude. I could not help but groan. The relief, when it was over, was enormous.

Chris, at that moment, was in another part of the house. But she must have heard me, for she came running over.

"Oh, Lonesome," she said. But her expression was not at all solicitous this time. Instead, it was filled with incredulous delight. "Look what you've got," she said.

She reached down her hand and picked up a limp, reddish creature not unlike a rather large mouse. I stared at it and sniffed at it, but was not at all impressed. It was wet and blind and helpless, and it made little grunting noises that were neither articulate nor particularly inspiring. And at that moment, the pains started again. There was another tremendous wrench, and a second mouse-like creature appeared. Twenty-four hours later, there were eight of them altogether, lying in an untidy heap beside me.

They were hardly handsome to look at. There were black ones, white ones, yellow ones, patchy ones, smooth ones and some that already exhibited signs of my own distinctive fuzzy-haired muzzle. And every single one of them was blind.

Chris, however, exhibited none of my distaste; she crooned and gibbered at them as if she had managed to create them all by herself. But there was an undercurrent of something else in her rapture; the only thing I could liken it to was dread.

Before they were more than a few hours old, her face hardened. Suddenly, she picked one up and rushed out the door. Immediately, the creature began to *kiyi* in a voice out of all proportion to its size. At once I felt obliged to rush and retrieve it, but as soon as I tried to move, I knocked all the other mice into a heap and they started yelling just as loudly, so I was forced to pacify them. In any case, the house door was now shut; there was the sound of the axe on the chopping block, and at once the *kiyi*ing stopped.

The moment Chris came back, she grabbed another. The same *kiyi*ing; the same foiled attempt on my part to follow; the same whack and sudden cessation of noise. Again she stormed through the door; and again. Finally, there were only two mice left. And Chris was doing something I had rarely seen her do before. It is a form of expression that seems peculiar to humans: her face reddened and screwed up into an agonized grimace; choking grunts issued from her throat; and a steady stream of tears flowed from her eyes. It was as if she had leaned over a smoky campfire and been caught unawares by the fumes, but it was puzzling because there was no hint of the smell of smoke on her clothes.

⁂

CANIDS WITH PUPPIES have strict rituals they are obliged to follow, and for the first four days I did not want to leave my offspring even for a moment. Chris had to literally drag me outside long enough to go to the bathroom. After that, however, the hormones clicked off, and I would not have cared very much if I had never seen the pups again. But having an inside bed was a privilege I was not about to readily relinquish, even though it was also tenanted by the two mewling, wriggling babies, who promptly climbed all over me and nuzzled a belly on which the sores from the ordeal with the ice had still not healed.

A few days later, Tan Sister and her pack returned home. It was time for Chris and me to go back up the river to our cabin.

The puppies had grown with amazing rapidity, and they were now the size of small cats. However, their eyes were still tightly closed, and their legs were so undeveloped they could barely lift their fat bellies off the ground. There was obviously no way they were going to be able to walk for a day and a half, and I assumed

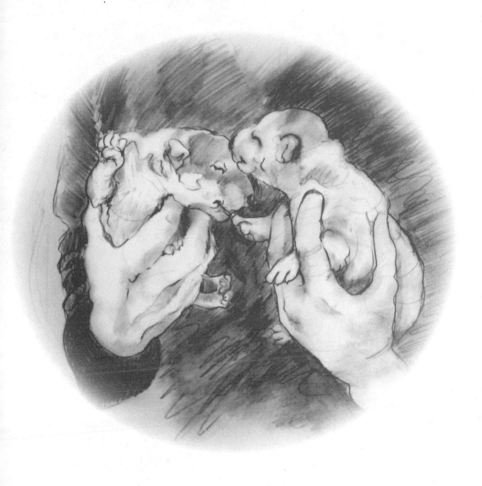

The puppies were now the size of small cats.

they were going to be left behind. I was not sorry, for they had begun to be a bit of a nuisance and gave me little time to myself.

Chris, however, did the oddest thing. Having placed her pack on her back, she slipped the two puppies inside her coat. And she kept them there the whole way home. Every so often, when we stopped for a break, Chris would slip her sleeping mat free from the straps that encircled her backpack, toss the mat on the snow for me to lie on and give me the puppies to suckle.

Well.

＊

I WAS NOT lucky with my children. When they were about two months of age, Chris took one of them out to Stuie with the idea of giving it away. Both she and the pup were exhausted from the journey—Chris left the baby beside a water bowl in the yard while she went into the house to get a drink for herself; a visitor drove in and ran over it, killing it instantly.

Chris had some idea of keeping the other, but despite the integrity of the father (and, I should add, my own irreproachable character), the puppy turned out to be a hysterical and yappy individual without a single grain of sense. He was nervous of humans and developed the habit of running behind them and nipping them on their heels. Nothing I said altered this deplorable and unnecessary habit. He was also inordinately frightened of children (who, I have to agree, are generally subhuman until they grow up, but one should not show any animosity toward them nonetheless). Chris began to be concerned that a child might be bitten.

Something began to weigh heavily on Chris's spirit. When the pup was 10 months old, the three of us went out to Stuie on one of our regular visits. Debbie and Michael had taken their pack back east for the winter (draining the waterbed before they left this time), and Chris stayed in the big house alone. Her face grew gloomier and gloomier; she hummed and sighed and snapped at me for every little thing. Finally, she walked over to the neighbours'. When she came back, to my utter horror, she carried that most execrable of objects, a carbon copy of the broom-shaped tool that had so discombobulated me at Simon's place that time. Its very smell filled me with dread.

Chris shut me in the house; there was a shot quickly muffled by the snow-laden trees. When Chris came back into the house, she was sniffing and weeping again, and the smells of gun oil, cordite and freshly turned earth clung to her clothes.

I never saw the puppy again.

CHAPTER NINE

CHRIS WAS PERENNIALLY HARD UP, so she took on occasional cash-paying jobs whenever they fitted into her lifestyle. One of these was the contract for painting all the picnic tables and outhouses in the park campgrounds, an activity that frequently earned the comment from people who knew her: "Oh, they need to hire an artist for that job now, do they?"

But one of the more memorable jobs was as a census taker. First, she had to take an examination. She got the highest mark of all the candidates, but at that time she was not yet a Canadian citizen. Thus the position was earned by an American woman who had been a Canadian for six months. Before Chris went back in the bush, however, the American woman called her. In extreme rural situations, all the paperwork has to be done by the enumerator—he or she must interview all the candidates personally and write out all the forms. The American woman wanted to "count" the people who lived off-road up our river—the homesteaders, Simon and Chris herself. There was also the hike-in campground near the lookout to Hunlen Falls to fit into the schedule. Whereas known individuals could be approached at any time, itinerants had to be caught on the prescribed date of June 2. Initially, the American woman looked at hiring Chris as a guide, but when she found that the round trip could take anything from three to five days, with no guarantee as to the timing, she balked. The upshot was that Chris was hired as a special enumerator specifically for the four off-road residents and the Hunlen Falls campground. After the necessary week's training (designed especially for off-road enumerators—most of the other people on the course would do their counting from fishboats and even kayaks), she headed back upriver.

Late May and early June in these mountains is the time of peak spring runoff. And that year was a dilly. The snow at higher levels had been heavy; April and May had been cool, but right at the end of the month there had been a sudden, blazing hot spell, and the runoff was spectacular. The tote road was completely awash for a mile and a half—we had to leave the truck quite close to the highway and wade through the overflowing river on foot. For much of the time the water was up to Chris's knees. I spent a lot of time scrambling on the steep rock slides above it, but an inevitable amount of swimming was necessary, and that pleased me, as you can imagine, not one bit. What sacrifices one makes to do one's duty for one's nation!

We had to be at the Hunlen Falls campground that night. Chris did not think we had time to detour to Simon's place on the same day, so she was going to catch the old man later. But by sheer chance, Simon happened to be going out to Bella Coola, and we met him on the trail.

"I'm doing the census," Chris bellowed after the usual greetings were past. "I'm supposed to count you. I can catch you later if you want. But do you want to do it now?"

Well, Simon had no problem with that, so they sat down right then and there on a log, and Chris roared out the questions. Off-road inhabitants never fit very well into standard government forms. Chris was particularly amused, I remember, when she asked for the square footage of Simon's dwelling. The answer was "64."

Instead of paddling up the Stillwater after interviewing Simon, as we would have done if we were going straight home, we stayed on the tourist trail that led to the Hunlen Falls campground, the trail I had tried to walk up the first time we came into the valley.

I often heard people speak about these falls—they were famous for their 1,000-foot drop—and we had visited them several times, hanging on by our toenails (or in Chris's case, her fingernails) to the trees and rocks of the sloping viewpoint that perched at the top of a mighty chasm. The falls fell straight as a ribbon down a rock face at the head of this canyon.

The trail was long and the hike was thirsty work. The campground was situated a half-hour's walk away from the falls, and when we arrived we dumped our packs in one of the tent sites. There was, as I had privately predicted, no one there, although to my surprise there were scents and footprints that showed us we were by no means the first party to travel up to the campground that year. It was a beautiful evening, clear and absolutely still, with a coolness that promised a frost. The lake was a mirror; the songs of varied thrushes rang like telephone bells into the clear, windless air.

The water monster is generally in a grumpy mood as a result of the traumatic experience it has to go through when plummeting down the cliff face, and it often shrouds itself with fog in the morning. But when we visited the falls this time, the early-morning sun was poking long yellow fingers into the canyon, and chips of rainbows were flung carelessly about the billows of spray. The bottom of the falls was hidden by the remnants of a massive snow cone that reared like a sugary phallus from the canyon's rocky floor.

Chris had made arrangements with the man who operated the campground to hire one of the canoes he kept there, and we spent a happy hour paddling up the lake to connect with an old surveyor's trail that would take us down to Lonesome Lake. (There is now a good hiking trail linking the two routes, but at the time we did the census, it had not been built.) By early afternoon we were home, and Chris collared the homesteaders and dutifully recorded their incomes and assets. Finally, she retired to her own place and wrote out the forms for herself.

Completing the forms, however, was only part of the job. They still had to be handed in to the authorities. They could not languish at Lonesome Lake until the next mail trip came along, so Chris had to return to the road at once.

In normal times, the quickest way to reach the highway would have been to stay along the valley bottom as we usually did. Even in the best years, however, crossing Hunlen Creek at the foot of Lonesome Lake could be a problem during high water, and it seemed very likely that we wouldn't be able to get over it at all that year. So Chris figured it was safer to go out the way we had come in, up and around by the top of the falls. Early the following morning, we climbed up the surveyor's trail, canoed back to the campground (where we did not stop this time) and plunged down the tourist trail to the footbridge. Having "counted" Simon on the way up, we could now head straight for the truck. Just before we hit the footbridge, we met a couple of hikers coming up the trail. After struggling along the flooded tote road, they thought they were heading into the epitome of wilderness. They expressed considerable surprise at seeing another human being.

Ever aware of the drama of a situation, Chris played her audience well.

"Where are you from?" she asked.

"Ontario," came the reply.

"Where did you spend Tuesday night?"

The hikers looked a little dubious. "By the road," said one of them cautiously.

"Sleeping in the car," said the other.

"Well, I'm the census taker," Chris grinned, whipping out her forms, "and I guess I had better get you counted."

You should have seen the look on their faces.

~

ONE THANKSGIVING, BELLA Coola was buzzing with news. "Buttons are fetching 50 bucks!"

"Buttons?" said Chris.

"Number ones!" was the reply.

They were talking about mushrooms. Pine mushrooms. They are (I gathered from the excited conversations) enjoyed with something akin to reverence in Japan, where, after being airfreighted to that country, they are sold for four or five times the price given to pickers in Canada. Chris, ever ready to give a lecture, liked to expound to anyone within earshot that "pineys" could not be raised artificially, so when their habitat was destroyed, the mushrooms disappeared as well. She said that Europe used to have them until their forest practices destroyed the old growth, and now the main crop usually came from Korea. It was the failure of the Korean crop that had boosted the prices in British Columbia that year.

Chris, at that point (despite her inclination toward avarice), did not at once rush out into the bush and see what she could find. On the whole, she despised the pickers; the mushrooms grew under carpets of moss on the forest floor, and pickers, hundreds of whom came from outside the valley, often destroyed the fragile ecosystem to get at them. Many of them also left a legacy of candy wrappers, lunch bags and pop cans in their wake. Besides, there was that long

116

walk to town to get to the mushroom buyers—and anyway, what did the darn things look like?

But—50 bucks a pound!

To give Chris her due, she gave it little more thought until, walking along the game trail behind the house a day or two after she had returned home, she was brought up short by a scattered patch of large white toadstools. The expression on her face was at once a mixture of surprise, caution, hopefulness and avidity. "I dunno, Lonesome. What do you think? Are these the right ones?"

Well, I was hardly the best person to ask, toadstools being practically rock bottom on my list of interests. But as Chris was examining them so closely, I gave them a more detailed look. As fungi go, these were huge. The largest, which was fully open, had a top as big as a dinner plate. Halfway down its long, thick, rubbery stem were the remains of a little frill. "A veil; that's correct," Chris murmured. "White gills; strong, earthy smell . . . hmmm."

"It's only the buttons that are fetching 50 bucks," she explained to the homesteaders later that day as we went over the river to collect our daily ration of milk. "They're the ones with unbroken veils."

"Sounds somewhat virginal," giggled Kathleen shyly.

Chris laughed. "There are five grades," she explained. "Twos have a partially intact veil, and fives are the big open ones. Even they're fetching 12 bucks a pound, and some of those big ones must be a pound apiece. Money just lying around waiting to be picked. I think I'll make another trip straight back out to Bella Coola. Even a backpack load should bring me in quite a bit."

There was a pause in the conversation, and the mood subtly changed.

"This is our property," said George. "If you pick our mushrooms, we should get something for them."

If Chris had possessed a tail, it would have stiffened.

"But I'll be the one packing them out, and if I hadn't told you about them, you would never have known."

If the homesteaders had possessed hackles, they would have risen.

"Oh well," said Chris a little disgustedly. "I don't doubt that I'll easily find more beyond your boundary." And off she went with a frown sitting heavily on her brow, leaving the patch behind the cabin intact. The homesteaders went to finish what they were doing and later brought a bucket to collect their loot. But every one of the mushrooms had disappeared. A short search revealed them stuffed into the forks of branches high up in the trees. The squirrels had gotten at them first and hung them up to dry so that they could store them in their middens and eat them during the winter.

THE FOLLOWING MORNING, Chris and I set off for Bella Coola again. Chris was carrying three boxes of mushrooms strapped to her backpack frame, some of which were the homesteaders' mushrooms; for these she was to receive half their booty.

But "the best-laid schemes o' dogs an' men gang aft agley" (to quote that famous master of doggerel, Rabbit Cairns), and at the foot of Lonesome Lake there was a hitch. Tacked to a tree was a square of paper. I was only just learning to read and might have had a problem with the message, but Chris mouthed the words out loud, so I was in no doubt as to their meaning.

DANGEROUS GRIZZLY.
GOT CHARGED BY SOW WITH TWO CUBS 13TH OCT.
ABANDONED PACK AND FOOD.

It was unsigned, but the only person who could have written it was Simon.

"Oh," said Chris. "A dangerous grizzly. Simon must have been mushroom picking, too. That was two days ago. What do you think we should do, Lonesome?"

—*Go home, of course*, I intimated disgustedly. —*Surely that's what anyone with any intelligence would do.* And I fully expected her to comply.

But even as I watched, the pupils of Chris's eyes did a curious thing. They wavered, stretched and began to curve until they resembled snakes with two vertical strokes going down the centre. "Ding!" she giggled foolishly. And our fate was sealed.

As you can imagine, travelling through the stretch of forest between the two lakes after reading that note was nerve-wracking to say the least. The salmon-spawning season was in full swing, and my nose registered dozens of bears. We saw no sign of Simon's abandoned pack and food. We did, however, see a grizzly. Both of us had a moment of pure terror in case it was The One. But this bear peered uncertainly at us from behind a tree and then carefully backed off and gave us a wide berth; luckily, she was just as suspicious of us as we were of her.

Simon was not at home for the simple reason that he was lined up with the other pickers at the buyers' place down in the Bella Coola Valley, and it was there that we were able to quiz him about his encounter.

"Yes," he intoned in his wheezy voice, combing his beard with his fingers. "I didn't even see her at first, but I heard this dreadful roar, and she came bounding through the bush, bellowing at every step. I dropped my pack and ducked behind a tree, and she kept going right past me toward the river. I got out of there in a real hurry, I can tell you. I went up the next day and got my gear, though. She hadn't even touched it."

"Scary," said Chris fervently, already dreading the journey home. And the other pickers chimed in with their stories of near misses with bears. But they were consoled by one indisputable fact. Buttons were now fetching 60 dollars per pound. Chris's share of her backpack load came to $460.

The upshot of all this was that Simon proposed to walk back up the stretch between the two lakes with Chris, carrying his rifle. "It's all right," he said when Chris protested. "I'm going to keep picking in that area anyway. I'll take a bucket with me and collect them on my way back home." And in fact, as it turned out, we saw no bears at all on that trip. It was obvious that Chris, and possibly even Simon, had no idea of the actual bear population of that short stretch of woods at salmon-spawning time. If they'd had a nose like mine, they would not have dreamed of setting foot there at all.

As we reached Lonesome Lake, another surprise was in store for us. I, needless to say, had registered it long before the humans; along the breeze that blew steadily from the lake came the scents of two other people and a plane. We had never before encountered anyone outside our small community on that lake.

"Goddamn it," said Chris. "They're picking our mushrooms."

"Oh, I guess there's enough for everyone," said Simon uncomfortably.

Nonetheless, he waited with Chris until the owner of the plane came back.

"Why do you have to come to this lake?" said Chris, who knew the man. "You can fly to any lake in the area. There's lots of uninhabited ones. We're limited by where we can walk and what we can carry on our backs."

"It's public land," sneered the pilot. (He was wrong there—it was Tweedsmuir Park. In fact, no one should have been taking mushrooms out of it at all, including Chris.)

"And what do you want to pick mushrooms for anyway?" said Chris heatedly. "You've got an expensive house and your own plane. You don't need the money."

"It gets me out into the bush," said the man, affronted.

"So the only time you go in the bush is when you can take something out of it! We're in the bush because we like to live in it. Not just take from it. Don't you know how to enjoy the bush for its own sake?"

"Come on," said the pilot's companion. "Let's go. We don't have to stay for this."

The pilot shrugged, but he obligingly got into his plane, and the two of them took off.

"You know," said Simon reflectively. "There's so many mushrooms in the area right now, and the price is so high, that it would almost pay us to hire our own plane. It would save lots of time backpacking them in and out. If George and Kathleen went in with us, it wouldn't cost that much each."

So that was what we did.

Thus followed an extraordinary week. Everyone spoke, thought, lived and breathed mushrooms from morning until night.

"Some pickers," Chris explained to the homesteaders, "use garden rakes to rip up the carpets of moss. That's where the buttons are hidden. By the time the cap pushes through the moss, it's already a number three or number four. But if you rip up the forest floor like that, you not only destroy the moss, but also expose the ground to drying, and that kills the network of threads, or mycelium, which is the main part of the mushroom plant." (You'll have to excuse me if I seem pedantic here, but I am quoting Chris verbatim, and this is the way she was.)

"The bit we see above the ground," Chris continued, "is only the fruiting body. Most mushrooms have complicated relationships with all the other plants in the forest. Their mycelium is so fine it can penetrate the cells in the root hairs of a plant—either a tiny weed or a huge tree. In return for extracting the plant's sugars, the mushroom feeds in a much greater percentage of water and minerals. It's a fantastic symbiotic relationship which occurs with most plants, not only in the forest but in the garden as well. One theory is that a forest is not a collection of plants, but one single organism all interlinked by the mushroom internet."

If this speech appears to be uninspiring, it was sheer high adventure compared with what went on during the following week. At first, setting off in the morning, it was as if we were going for a walk, and I would trot happily along, savouring the morning smells and thinking that life was pretty good. But as soon as we closed the little gate in the property fence, we halted at the first patch of moss. Then this is what Chris did, and I kid you not. She got on her hands and knees, crawled around and patted every single bump. Most of these concealed rocks or cones, but sometimes there were mushrooms underneath. I could have told her at once which bumps were profitable, just by using my nose. Nonetheless, Chris soon learned to distinguish between the rigidity of a rock and the springy resilience of a mushroom without having to look beneath the moss. Then she would carefully extract her prize and replace the moss.

You can imagine how tedious the whole business was for me. No sooner had we started walking than Chris would stop at the next patch and pat and fumble like a discombobulated raccoon.

Not all of the mushrooms grew beneath the moss. Some stood bold and plain upon the duff, and others grew among the stones on the dry ridges that poked up between the firs. Every gleam of white had to be investigated. Sometimes it turned out to be a stone or a bleached stick, but the buckets and boxes filled, and a couple of days later, the horses, the humans and I, all with packs loaded to capacity, went to meet the hired plane down on the lake. A friend of Simon's was to pick the mushrooms up from the float-plane base and deliver them to the buyer for us.

Most of the time during that mushroom-picking week, I dozed— keeping, nonetheless, a watchful nose out for bears. Their effluvium was always present to a greater or lesser degree, and in one heart-stopping moment we practically fell over a young male who was snoozing in a bed he had made for himself in the red duff of a rotten log. Fortunately, the bear was equally horror-struck, and he exploded from beneath our feet and galloped away as fast as his heavy, furry paws could go.

"You missed that one, Lonesome," said Chris reprovingly when she was able to speak again.

—There's not much I can do if the wind is wrong, I shrugged huffily. *—You've got to expect stuff like this. It is the bears' territory after all.* And I reflected wistfully, and by no means for the first time, upon the joys of suburban living.

A short time later, we were picking quietly not far from the river when a stick cracked in a nearby brushy gully. Chris froze, listening. I could not understand what was bothering her. A soft scuffle and another small crack. Chris looked wildly around for a tree. Nothing close by had a branch on it for 50 feet. Again she stopped, listened, stared. The soft scuff of leaves was getting closer.

Just as she was getting into a real blue funk, out of the bush walked George and Kathleen.

I can quite see why humans welcomed our ancestors into their caves. Without us, they would have followed the fate of the dinosaurs pretty quick.

CHAPTER TEN

ONE WINTER MORNING, GEORGE AND Kathleen informed Chris that they were putting their homestead up for sale. After nearly 40 years of subsistence living, they wanted to try something a little different. Chris had no idea if the new owners, whoever they might be and whenever they might appear, would allow her to stay, and she decided to look for somewhere else to live.

She was now 38 human years old; if she was going to start again (she frequently told me), she should do it soon while she still had the physical strength and energy. So the following spring, almost four years to the day since we had first walked up the river (which would make me five years old), we began the long process of packing Chris's enormous pile of possessions down to the lake. I learned from her conversations with George and Kathleen that the float plane would come in after the ice had gone out and fly the boxes up to the base, where they would be stored until Chris wanted them again.

I say "we" in the above paragraph because by that time I was backpacking, too.

This humiliation started after a visit to Stuie. I had heard the homesteaders tell Chris how they had made a little wooden cross-tree, just like a horse's packsaddle, for the dog they once owned (an animal who was, in some obscure way, a relative of mine), and how the dog would leap with excitement when the pack was produced, for it knew it was going for a walk. Poor thing; all it was probably responding to was the relief of being let off its chain. As I was almost never subjected to this indignity, I hardly needed the stimulation of further bondage to get excited.

In fact, whenever the pack was presented, I did my utmost to demonstrate how much I hated it, even degrading myself by crawling under bushes and grovelling. But instead of being sympathetic, Chris only got mad. "For Chrissake, Lonesome," she would snarl. "You're not a city dog. You've got to earn your keep." (As if I didn't already. Were not my nose and tail the best bear-warning devices ever invented?)

I had always loathed a collar and never, as a general rule, wore one. So when a pack was first put over my back, I writhed in panic. This happened at Stuie, and it was Debbie who held me; the backpack was a set of saddlebags that had been bought for an earlier dog of theirs, and they had no intention of using it on Tan Sister. Chris's strong hands flicked straps and buckles, and no matter how I wriggled, I was held fast. We walked to the neighbour's garden, which was only a few minutes away, and Chris and Debbie dug carrots (the vegetable which, of all of them, I despise the most) and then stuck a bunch into each of the saddlebags so that the feathery tops sprouted on either side of me like the plumage of a menacing bird.

"She looks so cute," Chris brayed. "Just like a Mexican donkey. Oh, Lonesome. You do look funny."

To be subject to the indignities of subservience was one thing; to be laughed at was inexcusable. I dragged my feet and made no effort to hide my disgust at the whole proceeding.

Once the pack was removed, I put it out of my mind, imagining that this was merely a cruel, passing game. Imagine my dismay, therefore, the following day when, after we had driven up the tote road, this loathsome object came out of the cab. What is more, it was now extremely heavy.

"Eight pounds, a dog your size is supposed to be able to carry," Chris said. "So I've given you two four-pound bags of sugar, one in each side."

That hike to Lonesome Lake was the most miserable I have ever made in my life. It wasn't so much the weight that bothered me, although that was bad enough, but the fact that I was suddenly much wider. I was totally baffled by the pack's bulging sides. When a stick touched them, I automatically stopped and waited for Chris to rescue me. But all she did was get madder and madder: "For goodness' sake, Lonesome. It's just a little twig. Stop being so feeble. Anyone would think you had no brains at all." And so on. By the time we reached the Stillwater, she was in the blackest of moods, which was not helping the situation one bit.

Just before we got to the canoe, the trail crossed a little gully spanned by an old fir log that we always used as a bridge. I was so unbalanced by the awkward weights on my sides that I slipped and fell in. Fortunately, there was no water in the gully, but I landed painfully on the rocky floor, adding a multitude of bruises to my already severely aching body.

But do you think Chris was sympathetic? Not a bit of it. Our packs came off in the canoe, of course, but as soon as we reached the next stretch of forest, on they went again; even my most earnest (and quite genuine) pathetic expressions made no impression on my hard-hearted human whatsoever.

I fought that pack for well over a year, running away and trying to hide every time I saw it. But Chris has a pig-headedness you wouldn't believe, and she never unbent a jot. Eventually, I decided I would have to make the best of it, although I never grew to like it.

*Humans accumulate an enormous amount of useless stuff; I've carried
a considerable number of strange objects in my pack over the years.*

But I learned to judge the width and weight of the packs with precision, and when we came to a fallen tree whose branches formed a network to the ground, barring my passage, I soon figured out how I could wiggle one side through first, then squirm and thrash until I could force the other to follow. Sometimes even that would not work, and I would look up the log, then down, to see if there was an easier way around. The type of country through which we habitually travelled was much laced with these kinds of obstacles, and I became very adept at negotiating them. Because I walked behind her, Chris was largely oblivious of the adroitness that I developed (although she would always wait and check on me when a particularly difficult obstruction presented itself), but the first person to walk behind me while I was packing at once expressed amazement at my prowess.

"You're missing most of this, Chris," he said, "but you should see how Lonesome figures out ways to get through some of this stuff. It's amazing how she works it out. This is a dog who thinks!"

Well, of course I think. How on earth can one get through this life without doing so? Flattery, however, is never unwelcome, no matter how condescending it might be. I hope Chris reads these words and takes due note.

Humans accumulate an enormous amount of useless stuff, and I've carried a considerable number of strange objects during my career. On hiking trips, there was the food, both mine and Chris's, the smoke-encrusted billycan (Chris always used to cook both her water, which she flavoured with various kinds of bitter powders, and her kibble), sometimes parts of the tent, extra clothes and even, on occasion, a rock or two that Chris, for some incomprehensible reason, decided I would have to carry home. After a visit to Bella Coola, there would often be tools, things like glue or chainsaw parts, to pack; and when a load of freight had been flown in, there was a multitude of items: nails, books, cans of sardines, chain oil, butter, dish detergent, putty, you name it—if it was small and heavy, I probably had to pack it at some time or other. (I never, let it be said, got to carry stuff like toilet paper.)

Fortunately, however, much of Chris's freight came in packages that were too large to fit into my pack. To help with those, the homesteaders sometimes brought their horses along (great big lumbering brutes who broke wind with every step), but during the summer, the horses were either busy with haymaking or grazing on a natural meadow some distance from home, and during much of the winter the trail was too icy for their hard, clawless feet. At those times (I am pleased to say), Chris had to carry all the bulky objects herself.

And so it was when we ferried her possessions back down to the lake. The preceding days had been an almost direct repeat of the time before we left Salmon Arm. There was the same chaos of paper, cardboard cartons and string—and the same increasing snappishness and ill temper.

Finally the stuff was all piled in the little shed by the wharf, and Chris and I hiked out to the road. And it just shows you how worthless all these objects were, for it was to be a surprisingly long time before we saw any of them again.

CHAPTER ELEVEN

WE WERE, IT TRANSPIRED, ABOUT to embark upon a very different adventure.

Early one morning, right after we turned our backs on Lonesome Lake, we drove upvalley and began to groan and grind up the tortured switchbacks of The Hill. It had been full spring in the valley, but at the top, snow lay thickly beside the road, just as it had done when we first drove this way. We did not stop on this occasion, although we called briefly at the float-plane base at Nimpo Lake (whose water was still frozen solid). After a while we drove out of the snow again and across the winter-tawny landscape of the Chilcotin. We reached Williams Lake, turned south and were soon bowling along the highway up which we had driven so long before. We did not retrace our route exactly, however, for a quieter road offered us a pleasanter ride eastward, and we eventually found ourselves crawling down another very long, steep hill. While it was by no means as tortuous as the one into the Bella Coola Valley, it was to afford me a moment of great terror.

The truck, already quite ancient upon my first acquaintance with it, was not getting any younger. Like my human, it had distinct eccentricities; recently, I am sorry to say, it had developed a most unpleasant ailment in its alimentary canal. Most of the time the affliction was in abeyance, but the long downward slope must have triggered some sort of rebellion in its bowels, for suddenly a series of tremendous gaseous eructations were unleashed right under the floor of the box. The bark of Simon's rifle, which had so discombobulated me before, was a mere rap of the knuckles compared with these mind-shattering detonations.

I was riding in the open back of the truck as usual. The cab was the kind that was equipped with sliding windows facing the box, which, on that warm spring day, were open. I hardly stopped to think; I leapt through the windows and onto Chris's lap. (I had not, you must realize, sat there since I was a very small puppy.)

Chris tried to push me off. "I can't see, Lonesome, you nitwit," she said. The truck wobbled dangerously toward the drop. However, there was absolutely nothing that was going to make me budge. Chris, flint-hearted creature that she was, started to laugh. She laughed so hard she had to stop the truck for fear that she would drive us off the road. But nothing would induce me to go back into the box until I was very sure that the digestive disturbance had been cured.

This long descent from the high interior plateau to the Thompson River Valley brought us once more through a dramatic change of climate, from winter into spring. "Ah, smell the cottonwoods," Chris iterated. But I, still piqued at my great fright and not a little humiliated by Chris's unsympathetic response, could see very little to be happy about; once we were on the flat, however, the bowel disturbance quietened down, and gradually I relaxed.

As usual, it was the slowing down and the bumping over a rough road that woke me. We had arrived at yet another lake; who would have guessed that there was so much Wet in this country of ours? This lake was surrounded by pale-trunked aspens decked in trembling veils of spring green. But the camping spot was very different from the ones Chris usually chose. It was absolutely full of people.

Dozens of them. Most were quite a bit younger than Chris; they were all tired and grubby, flamingly sunburned and dressed in a variety of ragged, filthy clothes. To my unutterable delight, Chris pitched her tent among this gaggle of humanity, and, joy of unmitigated joys, there was food. Huge quantities of human fodder, which meant tons and tons of leftovers. Meat, potatoes, carrots (which I left politely beside my plate) and banana cream pie. Even though there were two other dogs with whom to share the feast, I was able to gorge myself until I was ready to burst.

The next morning, everyone piled into a number of beat-up vehicles (which were referred to by the strange name of "crummies") and drove a short distance through rolling farmland and then into a section of forest.

But it was like no other forest I had ever seen. A tremendous disaster had happened here. Trees had been flattened, broken and burned, and an army of blackened, ragged stumps stretched as far as the eye could see. No animals remained—no insects, no birds, no mice. The only scents were those of the immolation: charred wood, scorched soil and ash.

The majority of the people began to take boxes out of the pickup trucks. Inside were thousands of small conifers that smelled of some highly unpleasant chemical. The people stuffed bundles of these plants into curious triple bags that were slung about their waists, somewhat reminiscent of my own little saddlebags, although of course they hung quite differently on the erect torso of a human. And Chris, to my bemusement, followed suit. There she was, with a set of those waist packs (hers were white and stiff and reeked of vinyl), with a bunch of green feathers sprouting from each flank. Why, I sniggered delightedly to myself (I was far too polite to say it out loud), you look just like a Mexican donkey!

Two young males were also similarly equipped with spanking new equipment and a plumage of trees, and the three of them stood around and waited while a fourth man showed them what to do.

"This is a little baby," he said, extracting a seedling and looking at his new recruits doubtfully. "If you don't treat it properly, it will die." The boss (for it was he) was a lugubrious man who obviously had very little faith in the selection of humanity that stood before him.

"If you plant it too shallow, the roots will dry out and it will die. If you plant it too deep, the stem will rot and it will die. If the roots are not pointing down, they will not form properly and the tree will die. If the stem is not upright, it will not grow straight and it will produce low-grade timber."

One of the male recruits began to look impatient. He had the body of an incipient Atlas and was (to put it kindly) somewhat conservative in his outlook on life. Upon meeting Chris in camp the night before, he had marched up to her, shaken her hand and said, "Hi. I'm Terry. I'm going to be a planter. You must be the cook." He was now curling his lip at Chris, already determined that an old woman as ancient as his mother had no place in a macho job like tree planting.

"You have to scrape whatever is on the surface of the block for a 30-centimetre-square patch and place the tree in the middle of it," the boss was explaining patiently. "Any duff touching the tree will rot it; any roots of competing plants will smother it; any ash from the slash burn that touches the leaves will scorch them. Removing the junk and baring the mineral soil is called screefing. Watch."

And he took a curious short, narrow-bladed shovel, swiped it sideways over the surface of the ground a couple of times, then speared it into the middle of the cleared patch of grey sand.

"Keep the convex side of the blade facing away from you. Wiggle the shovel back and forth to make a slot in the ground. Feed the roots down the back of the shovel; make sure they are straight; check the depth; remove the shovel and tighten the earth with your foot—so." And he gave a little jab with his heel in the dirt beside the tree. The seedling stood firm and straight as a soldier in its little patch of naked soil.

"The spacing's 2.7 metres on this block. Trees planted too close together are faults, as are missed spots; any of these deficiencies may be held against us when payment is made for the block. Concentrate on putting the trees into the ground correctly at this stage." He looked at us sadly. "Don't think about the money until you've mastered the technique."

But money, I am afraid, is what had drawn Chris and her fellow workers to this blasted landscape in the first place. Eagerly, the three rookies rushed into the black tangle of stumps and slash to try out their new game. Scrape the ground; stab the shovel; fumble for a tree in the bag; feed it into the slot; kick. Three steps. Check for the position of the seedlings already planted; scrape; stab; fumble; feed; kick. And on. And on. And on.

At first, I found the whole business quite entertaining; it was, after all, a type of walk, and for Chris to indulge in a crowded activity so at odds with her nature was intriguing. But, like mushroom picking or flower photography, it was far too slow to give me much in the way of exercise, and the overriding holocaustal destruction with its dearth of living smells provided no mental stimulation whatsoever. Moreover, the black ash that covered the ground multiplied the sun's heat a hundredfold, and the temperature soon became unbearable. At first I embraced the momentary coolness of the soil patches newly cleared by the planters, even going so far as to make one or two attempts to enlarge these beds so that I could stretch my belly against them. But these actions at once precipitated such violent human aphorisms as "Get off the procreating trees!" (or words to that effect), and it was not long before I headed back to the crummy and sought relief within its shade.

At the end of the day, the people were as black as the block. Faces smeared, arms and necks reddened by the sun, they flung their equipment into the crummy, then drove like maniacs back to camp. I was thrown with abandon about the back with the bags and shovels and empty tree boxes. Chris was tired, but no more so than she would have been after a day in the mountains at home, and her skin was already toughened by the weather, so she had been little affected by the sun. The two youths who started with her, however, were both burned brick red and exhausted.

"How many trees did you plant?" everyone was asked. It was upon this tally that their wage depended.

"Four hundred," said Chris, not without a touch of pride; the youths had managed only 350 apiece, much to Mr. Atlas's chagrin. But then the more experienced planters sang out their tallies: 1,200; 1,500; 1,950.

"But how . . . ? " said the beginners, aghast.

The old hands shrugged. "We've all been through it. It takes a while, three or four weeks for most people. But it'll come."

Three or four weeks, I thought, astonished. We're going to be here with all these people for three or four weeks? How incredibly, phantasmagorically wonderful! Suddenly I felt a great surge of excitement. Would we be getting more of that wonderful food? Visions of banana cream pies danced in my head.

But banana cream pie wasn't the half of it. I've never imagined such sustenance as I was to receive during the seven spring seasons we spent in tree-planting camps. Curries, chilies, soups, chicken, turkey, hamburgers, roast beef; oatmeal and bacon and eggs in the morning; bread dripping with butter or gravy; cold cereal and milk; buns; toast; sandwiches with cold meats and cheese; ice cream (although there was never much left of that: just a lick of the container as a rule); custards, cakes and cookies. After a day or two (I have to confess), my alimentary canal was in nearly as bad a shape as that of our truck.

Although I continued to go out onto the blocks quite often, they were usually such hideous and depressing places that I preferred to stay in camp. For me, therefore, by far the most important people during our periods with the tree planters were those who prepared the food. They were almost as varied as the meals they put before us. And you may be sure that I ingratiated myself with these talented humans as soon as was decently possible—and usually without difficulty, thanks to my excellent manners.

The first cook I became acquainted with was a female who worked single-handedly to feed all 50 people and three dogs in camp. She lived in a tent, like most of the planters, but worked in a little travel trailer that had been equipped with a couple of propane stoves, a hotplate and a sink. She was an energetic woman and undoubtedly a competent cook; she should have had an assistant, but she had an acerbic nature and no one could work with her for long, which was why she ended up having to do this immense job on her own. Nonetheless, she was perfectly reliable—as long as she didn't drink.

Every five or six days we had a day off; everyone else would head for town, but Chris had no love of cities, motels, parties, drinking and dope (all of which a great many of her companions indulged in), and she was far happier staying in camp on her own.

One morning, after the break, the kitchen trailer remained locked. There was no smell of bacon and eggs and oats and pancakes and toast and coffee to greet the rising planters, and no sign of the cook.

This lady had a boyfriend who was part of the planting crew; the two of them were noted drinkers. This time they had had a stand-up fight in a bar and had both been thrown in jail for the night. The cook came back somewhat chastened, but her work with the crew was at an end. Within a few days, she was replaced by a man whom I came to know well over the years. Mario, with his thinning black hair and drooping moustache, was the spitting image of a stereotypical Italian organ grinder (sans monkey). I was at once introduced to mouth-watering lasagnes, phyllos and spaghetti sauces, as well as things like devilled eggs and the most magnificent fish chowder it has ever been my privilege to savour.

But that was all in the future. After a week at the little aspen lake, a tremendous packing ensued, and I began to think I had misunderstood the notion that we were to be tree planters for several weeks. Not only were the individuals' tents and equipment put away, but also the huge communal cookshack, a building composed of tarps, two-by-fours and plastic film. It was dismantled and loaded into a truck. The shower trailer, the generators, the propane tanks and all the planting equipment had to be stowed into trucks and crummies. At first, this veritable orgy of packing alarmed me considerably; I never lost the feeling of impending doom whenever this happened in Chris's life. But soon I came to realize that this process was an integral part of a tree planter's existence. During the season, we led pretty much a gypsy life, travelling to all parts of the province and seeing all sorts of nooks and crannies of the country I had never dreamed existed. But they all had one thing in common: they were all situated in areas ravaged by holocausts.

Sometimes, though, we were lucky enough to camp or even work beside patches of forests that were still standing. Chris was no stranger to physical effort and was generally the first to be out of the crummy and away in the morning. This meant that our first run of the day was often beside these stretches of untouched trees, and I loved to trot alongside Chris at these times, for here were forests burgeoning with growth and creatures that were always of interest. They were not, however, universally benign, as you will shortly see.

One cool morning, Chris was the first to be bagged up and away, as usual, and we started to work alongside a piece of living forest. Chris had picked up considerable working speed by that time—partly because she had learned to telescope the separate actions of the planting ritual (using one hand to stab with the shovel while the other was already reaching for a tree) and partly because she now had no trouble reading the ground. The bewilderment that all beginners feel when they have to spot the previously planted trees and correctly space their own seedlings, no matter how rough the terrain, suddenly disappears after three or four weeks. It is then that the planter's numbers dramatically jump. So Chris was pounding along with confidence, enjoying the sun and her dexterity and the coolness of the living forest close by. I was skipping happily along among the trees, investigating everything I saw.

Suddenly, I was confronted by an animal about the size of a very large cat. Its hair, however, was quite different, being long and extremely coarse. It was sitting on its haunches on the ground beneath a tree, paws clasped in front of its chest, its bulbous nose waffling.

We did not have these animals at Lonesome Lake, but I'd seen one not more than two days earlier. We had been driving back to camp when someone in our crummy said, "That pickup's been at the end of that logging road for over a week. Do you think we ought to investigate in case something's wrong?"

At which the driver flipped the wheel and lurched up a side road, and we stopped beside the pickup in question. The vehicle was not quite as pristine as it had at first seemed. As we noted the flattened tires and rust-streaked body, something moved inside. A shaggy-maned head reared over the steering wheel and glared at us.

"God!"

"Wow!"

"It's eaten all the seat covers."

"This truck is totally stripped!"

"That's the biggest porcupine I ever did see!"

I would have liked to investigate the strange new smell emanating from the animal, but with much laughter the planters turned the crummy and continued to camp.

Now, here in front of me, was another representative of this species. It must have been a young one, for it was much smaller than the one we had seen in the pickup. I approached it courteously and with deference, as I did with most of the creatures I met, but just as I was gently extending my nose to touch the animal, an unprecedented thing happened. It suddenly whirled round and rudely shoved its backside in my face. This form of attack had the most unexpected and painful results. It was as if a thorn bush had suddenly got up and jumped at me. What was worse, the thorns stayed firmly in my nose; I could neither shake them loose nor rub them away with my paw.

At first, Chris didn't notice anything amiss; she merely concentrated on her planting and spoke to me occasionally without looking my way. But then something must have alerted her; suddenly she did a double take. "Oh, Lonesome! Now look what you've got yourself into." She called me over, put one hand under my chin and then, with the other, tried to grasp one of the thorns. But the pain was at once intense, and I instantly wriggled free. Chris caught me easily enough again, but as soon as her hand moved near my face, I was gone. "Oh, well," she shrugged. "We'll have to wait until we go back to camp and I can get some help."

"TAKE THEM OUT with a pair of pliers."

"Leave them alone and they'll dissolve."

"Cut the ends off, and that'll take away some of the pressure."

"If you leave them, they'll work their way inside and might go into her eyes or brain."

"Take her to the vet."

"But," said the boss, looking at me with his mournful spaniel eyes, "if you want to get to a vet, we're going to have to radio for a barge to get us back across the reservoir"—we were working beside the dammed Columbia River north of Revelstoke—"and that's going to take quite a while to organize. We certainly can't do it before tomorrow, and then there's no vet in Revelstoke. You'll have to drive all the way to Salmon Arm. Then we'd have to get you back. We'll be out of here in three more days, and I don't know if the logging company'd let us have an extra barge under those circumstances. At best you'd miss three days of planting."

Chris looked at me speculatively. "Maybe we can get them out ourselves," she said. "I can't hold her on my own." She turned to the first-aid man, one of the few humans in camp who was of an age similar to her own. "Perhaps you could help me."

Well, I don't know who was more nervous, the first-aid man or me. His hands trembled so much he could barely hang onto me, and Chris's attempts with the pliers got her nowhere. Couldn't she understand that her efforts to be helpful were far more painful than the pricks had been in the first place? In the end, she had to admit defeat.

"I've managed to cut all the ends off," she said. "It must have been a small porcupine, because the quills are tiny. Thank goodness she's so gentle with animals. She must have just touched it with her nose. The quills are all concentrated in the end of it. I guess I'll just have to keep an eye on her. If she looks as though she's getting sick, I'll take her out; otherwise I'll let her see if she can get rid of them on her own."

At which I was released, and I trotted thankfully to my dinner, which had been interrupted.

"Huh," snorted the first-aid man disgustedly. "The way she's shoving her food round her dish, she's not feeling any pain."

And in truth, now that I had been let alone, I soon recovered. But I had added porcupines to my list of acquaintances and had learned to leave them very well alone.

It was another animal I encountered during our tree-planting adventures that affected me the most adversely. It was normally an innocuous animal, but it was to give me a close brush with death.

We often had contracts in the same areas year after year. One of the places we frequently camped at and usually for a number of weeks—was a small lake a few miles north of Kamloops. It was at a high elevation; the lake was generally frozen to a greater or lesser degree when we arrived, and snow and storms were common during our times there. (Why Chris always gravitates to these miserable climates is a mystery to me.)

This was where we moved after leaving the little aspen-ringed lake, and as soon as I got out of the truck, I received a most wonderful surprise.

Squeakers!

They were everywhere. We never had any at Lonesome Lake,

and I had all but forgotten about them, but the moment I heard that piercing whistle, the springs of puppyhood were invigorated, and I was off!

Chris didn't approve of me chasing any animal, but the squeakers knew it was just a game; they knew to a T how close they could let me get before diving down their holes, flicking their little scuts of tails as they went.

Chris's normal antisocial tendencies made it difficult for her to associate with people for too long a time, and for her, camp life was more than a little crowded. Besides, she never drank alcohol or smoked tobacco or marijuana, and she found, like me, the volume of noise from the tape deck too painful for the ears. The constant drones from the generator and water pumps were also irritating to her, and she claimed that the only way she could get any sleep was to remove herself as far as she could. So she always pitched her tent some distance away from everyone else.

I did not, needless to say, share these aberrant attitudes, and in the evening, after Chris had gone to her tent, I would stay beside the cookshack, sometimes begging for an occasional tidbit (although I certainly didn't need it; it was pure greed, and I would never have dared do it if Chris was around, but what the eye doesn't see . . .), sometimes watching the other dogs chase a Frisbee (I could never understand the point of that kind of inelegant cavorting and prostrating) and occasionally following some of the planters to the upper end of the lake, where they liked to go fishing. Fishing itself was of no great interest to me, but the attraction of this particular location was a simply enormous colony of squeakers that lived just across the road. I would sit with my back to them at first, pretending to watch the pale fly lines whip across the water, or the beaver who came out every evening and drew a silver wake across the lake.

Then, when I knew the ground squirrels were fooled, I would leap around and charge at them, revelling in the chorus of squeaks and whistles and the precipitate scramble for the holes.

One day after supper, I noticed the fishermen pick up their rods and head up the lake, and I happily trotted along behind. As always, I sat still with my back to the action and watched the fishing for a while, but when I judged the scenario behind me to be to my liking, into the colony of squeakers I whirled.

That evening, however, the chase took a somewhat different turn. One of the ground squirrels dived down a much larger hole than usual—a hole that was big enough for me to follow the squirrel into. A fair amount of Wet was running through the bottom of the hole, but the headiness of the chase precluded caution, and into its maw I went. The water might have deterred me, but the hole was in fact a tunnel, whose farther exit was plainly visible. I took my first euphoric leap into the one end just as a perky tail and hindquarters flicked out through the moon-round hole at the other.

Three-quarters of the way along the tunnel, my feet no longer hit hard metal. They began to sink into soft, accumulated silt. I started to panic; the water suddenly seemed much swifter than I had thought. I did not think I could go back the way I had come. I struggled ahead, but the silt deepened rapidly. With only two leaps to go, I was stuck.

The water was now horrifyingly powerful. It piled behind me, driving into the fur beneath my tail, and began to swoosh right over my back and shoulders.

I could hear the fishermen just a few yards away. Desperately, I tried to let them know I needed help. Being an intelligent dog, I didn't attempt to bark (I knew they would not understand dog-speak), but tried instead to imitate human noises to alert them to my perilous condition.

"Hey," said one of the fishermen after a moment. "What's that peculiar groaning noise?"

I gave another snuffling moan.

"Sounds like some critter in the culvert," said his friend. I could hear him coming closer.

"Watch that it isn't a skunk," the first fisherman laughed.

"There's none up here, surely," the other stated. "Maybe it's a beaver or a muskrat. Let's see if we can kill it."

And his cautious face suddenly loomed in the opening of the culvert.

"God," he said, jumping up. "Get your shovel. It's Lonesome. She's got herself stuck."

At once, his companion ran back to camp, yelling, "Give me a shovel. Give me a shovel, quick." Brandishing the tool like a sword, with a trail of excited people following after him, he liberated me back into the world.

Chris, meanwhile, was oblivious to all this, for her tent was in the other direction and far beyond earshot of all of the excitement. But when she came to breakfast the following morning, she heard the account of my adventures. "Well, Lonesome," she said severely. "That explains the mud on your flanks. Perhaps that will teach you to leave ground squirrels alone."

—*It wasn't the squirrels that were the problem*, I stated grumpily, —*but The Wet.*

I knew in my heart that she was right; however, there was something about that delectable whistle that I have never been able to resist. It speaks of springtime and all the carefree days of youth and the good times we had before I had ever heard of the wilderness.

But I had certainly learned to treat culverts with a great deal more respect.

CHAPTER TWELVE

I HAD BEEN NAIVE ENOUGH to assume that the removal of Chris's baggage from Lonesome Lake signalled the end of our wilderness life, and that we were now to settle down into a more conventional existence among our fellow dogs. For a while, this fantasy was encouraged. After that first tree-planting season, although we did some more travelling, we always returned to highways, buildings and all the comfortable paraphernalia of the civilized world. I had a great time visiting and recounting our adventures (which were somewhat more pleasurable in retrospect—I must confess to no little degree of gratification at the effect they aroused in my listeners). We stayed down at Stuie once in a while, but Debbie and Michael had taken Tan Sister and their son away; I heard Chris talk about a place called The Arctic, which was apparently very dismal and cold. Tan Sister, it appeared, was forced to be tied up there, as were all the dogs in the settlement. Many of the dogs were quite vicious; nonetheless, they apparently formed a remarkable choir that was conducted twice a day by a siren. Tan Sister auditioned for this august gathering and was successful enough to acquire a small part, which, when we were united again some years later, she would demonstrate ad nauseam.

At the end of the summer, I was somewhat disconcerted to see a number of the boxes of supplies accumulating again (they had been taken from the float-plane base at the end of the tree-planting season and stored at Stuie), particularly when Chris's chainsaw was unearthed and both it and the canoe were loaded once more onto the truck. (The alimentary canal of this ancient behemoth was still subject to spasms of outrageous flatulence in the most embarrassing of places.)

You can imagine the apprehension that visited me as I climbed aboard, for the salmon were already starting to spawn, and bear season was at its prime; it was not the most ideal time to head out into the bush. But instead of turning onto the tote road that would have taken us to Lonesome Lake, we climbed the switchbacks up The Hill back onto the Chilcotin Plateau. This was a route we had taken often through the summer, and I began to relax a little; perhaps we were simply going on another short jaunt, or maybe even going back to tree-planting camp. But why was she taking the chainsaw? Perhaps it was sick, and she was packing it out to the small-engines vet in Williams Lake. We would reach that town in about six hours; the direction we chose after that would give me a better idea of what we were going to do.

But town, I am afraid to say, was the last thing on Chris's mind. An hour or two east of the top of The Hill, we turned onto the inevitable bush road (which was rough, but nothing as bad as the tote road) and eventually climbed up to yet another lake. There, a man was waiting for us, and he helped Chris unload and launch the canoe and place some of the boxes in the centre, upon which both of them wobbled aboard and began to paddle along the lake. I knew the man slightly. Chris and I had bounced along his rough driveway and visited him at a large house containing two children and an adult female; their pack included cats and horses, too.

"Come on, Lonesome," Chris called. "It takes her a while to cotton on to the water bit," she confided to her companion. "For a dog that's so smart in other ways, she always falls apart when I get into a canoe."

Now this was grossly unfair. Humans seem unaware that when they go onto the water, their scent trail is broken, and it is very difficult for dogs to maintain olfactory contact with them. It's not so bad if the land route is one I am familiar with, but in strange country I inevitably feel a panicky sense of abandonment. Despite Chris's scathing comment, I had become used to most of her idiosyncrasies by now, and having watched to see which direction she was taking, I commenced to run along the shore. As long as she stayed within a few canoe lengths of land, I felt comparatively safe; I heard her advising the man (who was in the back and therefore steering) that they should not go too far out into the water.

The forest here was very different from that of the wetter, more coastal climate in which I had spent most of my life to date. Up here, most of the trees were brittle, rough-barked and long-needled, and interspersed with scrubby tufts of stunted, frost-bleached herbs and grasses. In wetter hollows, a prickly, tight-growing spruce abounded; in these areas there was much evidence of the huge, humped, horse-like creature the humans called "moose." To my cautious relief, however, there was not so much as a hint of salmon, and therefore no great concentration of bears.

A couple of miles along the lake, we rounded a little point and before us appeared a small cabin. The scent of the man in the canoe and his pack clung faintly to this building, but it was obvious that none of them had visited it for quite some time. The logs had weathered as golden as the frost-bleached grasses and as grey as the brittle pine branches that enclosed it. I was, needless to say, beginning to have a certain amount of trepidation about the venture by this time; when the equipment and the chainsaw were unloaded, my misgivings were confirmed. However, to my surprise, it was the man who picked up the chainsaw. He started to fall some of the dead trees and do some general maintenance about the place. Now this was more like it. Like many animals, humans evince certain types of behaviour relevant to their gender, of which the male taking charge of the machines is typical. Had Chris finally relinquished some of her dominant female status sufficiently to find a mate? Was I finally going to have a proper pack, like a dog is supposed to?

But my hope was short-lived. As the sun shone low and blinding on the water, we canoed back to the truck (with me riding inside the boat this time), and the man got into his own vehicle and drove away. I thought of the woman and children in his house and somewhat belatedly remembered that humans aspire to monogamy (although there are numerous exceptions to this rule) and that the man's farewells were casual and without, I regret to say, the characteristic touching that signifies pair bonding among the human species.

As the sun dropped lower and a nip of frost chilled the air (there had been thin fingers of ice in the shallows that morning), Chris piled an enormous load into the canoe and began to swing once more into the lake. It was very quiet; a loon called, the water whispered against the paddle, and the grey dusk fell. Suddenly, a tremendous feeling of loneliness washed over me. Sadly, I watched the canoe draw slowly away. Chris was smiling happily to herself, that same smile I had noticed so many times before at the start of long periods of solitude. With a heavy heart, I began to follow.

🖋

SNOW FELL, THE lake froze, and winter came. But in truth, things were not as bad as they might have been at this new location, which was known as Miner Lake. The hike to the road was comparatively easy, being mostly on the logging road, and it was possible to get to the nearest house (which belonged to the man who had come to

148

the cabin with us) in a matter of hours. Sometimes we would stay there overnight while Chris attended to her mail; if the weather was good, we often did the whole round trip in a single day. There were no bears to worry me; it was cold—much colder than at Lonesome Lake—but the snow was not excessively deep.

One day, Chris skied among some thickets of spruce and stopped beside a tangle of red willow around which rabbit tracks abounded. She took from her pocket a roll of hair-like wire that glinted golden in the winter sun. She fashioned it into a loop and suspended it between some bushes right above a little rabbit highway. The next day, when we returned, I was considerably excited to see that a rabbit was wearing the wire loop somewhat in the manner of a dog collar and chain; however, the animal was quite dead. (Is it any wonder that I hate collars so much?) Now, I had often tried to catch rabbits, but without success; they don't seem particularly intelligent, but they have a whole network of boltholes into which it is impossible for a dog to squeeze. So when Chris's curious device held the creature so securely, I was impressed. And when Chris shared a smidgen of the resulting stew with me, I was ecstatic. It was absolutely the best meal I'd ever had, even beating anything I had eaten in tree-planting camp. We did not eat rabbit all that often—sometimes the snares were empty—but such feasts were undoubtedly the highlights of that winter.

Another advantage of the place was that we were blessed with a human neighbour. The nature of our meeting with this individual was a little unusual.

Quite early in the winter, we had been out for a few days, staying with friends. The snow had deepened appreciably since we had left, but a snow-machine track facilitated our progress on the logging road. To our surprise, it turned onto the lake and ran all the way to the cabin.

I could, of course, smell at once that someone had been inside. Not only visited, but spent the night; there were aromas of cooked food and woodsmoke and whiffs of oil, blood, fur and a rather intriguing fishy scent. Chris was a little slower on the uptake. "Hmm," she said. "Footprints to and from the door, and the split wood by the stove has snow on it—it must have been done after the stove cooled. And look at the radio, Lonesome. It's not on the CBC anymore, but tuned to a country-and-western station. Someone," she said, turning to me and rolling her eyes theatrically, "has been staying here!" (Chris was an avid reader of detective mysteries, and I think she felt quite pleased at achieving this little piece of deduction.)

She did not seem unduly perturbed by the occurrence. (Her mother, however, when Chris later informed her of the incident by letter, reacted differently. She was, to put it mildly, horrified. "Fancy that man using your cabin without your permission!" she wrote back. "What a good thing he did not arrive when you were there and in bed!" But I digress.)

A day or two after we had returned to the cabin, my ears were visited by the distant but unmistakable whine of a snow machine; after a while, Chris also lifted her head and looked along the lake. She was smiling as the man stopped the motor and climbed off the machine. "Tea water's boiling," she sang out. (Tea drinking was, I believe, one of the habits in which the natives of her own country indulged. I have long since come to the conclusion that a lot of Chris's odd behaviour patterns have evolved because of her foreign upbringing; England must indeed be a strange country to live in.)

But the man, it appeared, was also enamoured of tea. He introduced himself as Arnold Capoose; he held the rights to the trapline.

"My cabin's another four mile farther on," he said in a voice so soft that many of the consonants were barely expressed. "An' it was dark and too tough to break trail, so I hope you don' min' me using the cabin."

"Of course not," Chris laughed. "Here. Help yourself to bread and cheese."

"I'm goin' to put sets in that beaver house along the lakeshore," Arnold said, leaning back in the cabin's only chair. The cabin was ill lit, and on mild days such as this the door was left open, so I had no trouble seeing inside. Chris was perched cross-legged on the rough pole bunk.

"I've seen the tracks where they've dragged aspens off the bank above the lake," she said. "I wouldn't have believed how high they've climbed to get food."

"Oh, they drag food quite a ways, all right." Then Arnold chuckled. "You gotta be careful setting traps in beaver houses. The animals swim aroun' under the water and keep the ice thin. I was setting that house las' year, an' I jus' got the post in an' fell right through up to my armpits. It was col' too. An' my brother, he was with me. An' he laugh' an' laugh'." Arnold's broad, comfortable body was also shaking with mirth as he told his tale.

"Well," grinned Chris, "at least if you fall in today, you'll have a warm cabin to dry out in."

But after Arnold left, he didn't return that day, so presumably his efforts went without incident. Over the ensuing weeks, however, every time he checked the sets he dropped in for tea. He never seemed to actually catch anything at the beaver house ("They're smart!" he would say admiringly), and I think Chris was secretly glad. She hated the idea of the animals being drowned in their own home, but she did appreciate Arnold's need to make his living off the land in a way that was close to the traditions of his people. "Very few people who work with nature," she would say severely to disapproving city friends, "have the right kind of education to make ready cash by things like writing. You can't expect people like Arnold, or me for that matter, to work in a factory or stock shelves in a supermarket. It would be worse than being in jail."

One day, Chris followed the snow-machine trail farther along the valley and skied to Arnold's cabin. Like most trap shelters, it was a crude shack with an earthen floor, and it was barely larger than a dog kennel. Arnold's bed was merely a thick pile of spruce boughs covered with a sleeping bag; the remaining floor space was dominated by a small upright oil drum out of whose side a square slab had been cut to form an ill-fitting door. Through the grinning maw of a crude damper chiselled below it, a fire glowed redly.

Arnold boiled the kettle and handed out oily, flesh-coloured slabs of a food that I knew at once were the origin of the fishy odour with which I had come to associate him. It was chinook salmon that his family had caught from the Chilko River and smoked. Chris loved this stuff and couldn't get enough of it; fortunately, humans are picky eaters, and they tossed the wonderfully greasy skins to me.

So a visit with Arnold was always a treat, but as with so many of the pleasurable things in my life, they were of a lamentably brief duration. The snow began to soften, and patches of bare ground appeared; when the pussy-willow buds were fat upon the bushes, Chris and Arnold went out together, slewing the truck with great difficulty over the logging road, which was by now losing its frost and had degenerated into an appalling bog. We dropped Arnold off at his summer home, and Chris and I went out to another tree-planting camp for a second season of planting.

We returned to Miner Lake when the ice had gone in July, and I assumed we would resume life much as we had done before. But once again, to my initial disbelief (although you might think I

would have known better by that time) and my later weary accep-
tance, yet another furious packing of possessions ensued. Chris's
temper was soon typically ragged, and load by load the worthless
accoutrements she had so laboriously taken there were paddled
back up the lake and piled into the truck.

What's with this human? I thought in despair. Is she never to be
satisfied? Are our lives going to be a series of endless packings and
moves from one unfriendly bit of real estate to another? Can't we
have a normal home with warm soft beds, nice neighbours to play
with and the proper social structure of a pack like everyone else?
Where oh where are we going to end up this time?

CHAPTER THIRTEEN

THIS EXPEDITION WAS OBVIOUSLY GOING to be of great magnitude. One would have thought that we already had enough possessions, but a formidable amount of shopping was done in Williams Lake. This necessitated several journeys to town and back, and I well remember one ghastly trip when the temperature must have reached a hundred degrees, and I thought I was going to collapse from heat exhaustion. The truck did; we had to wait for several hours beside the Fraser River until the day cooled enough for us to climb the long hill up onto the Chilcotin Plateau. But the most ominous portent of what was in store for me was the fact that all this freight was once more deposited at the float-plane base at Nimpo Lake; we were obviously destined for another fly-in/bush-bashing location a very long way from anywhere. Chris's fixation with wilderness living seemed to have reached manic proportions.

So I was very apprehensive when we turned off the highway onto yet another logging road, which on a scale of one to ten (with the tote road to Lonesome Lake being the worst) rated perhaps eight-and-a-half or nine. It was only moderately rocky—that wasn't its problem—but its speciality was a series of enormous puddles, many of which were so deep the water welled up through the rust holes in the floor of the cab. The truck ploughed through these like a hippopotamus doing a belly flop, but to give it credit, despite its noisy bellowing it must have done something to soothe the water monster, for it never once got stuck.

At the end of the road—the literal end—we pulled off as far as we could into the trees. Out came the packs; I resigned myself to the discomfort of the straps and buckles around my chest and belly, and off we started up the trail.

And a real trail it was to begin with. It climbed determinedly up a sparsely pined ridge with a small but noisy creek dashing along in a little steep gully below. A number of horses had used the track in the past and also a few trail bikes; traces of people on foot, however, were rare. There were bear scents, both black and grizzly, and the effluvia of wolf, pine martens, squirrels, moose and deer. But most smells were old, for the snow was not long departed; as usual, we were the first travellers forging our way into the wilderness that year.

Where the land levelled out at the top of the gully, I was heartily depressed (although not greatly surprised) to see the trail disappear. We commenced a terrible bush-bash through swampy spruce that clawed at our packs and faces. The early piquancy of the morning gave way to a warm, windless, humid greyness, an absolutely perfect climate for mosquitos. Their numbers and ferocity were unbelievable. I'd never experienced them to that degree either at Lonesome Lake or at Stuie. Chris cursed and swore and groaned and moaned and flapped a leafy willow branch against her face, but she never once intimated that she might return to a saner environment. I was forced to endure all this with my usual stoicism, despite having no means with which to keep the flies off my face. I was soon badly bitten on the nose and around the eyes.

After a while we came to an enormous swamp with so much Wet sitting in it that Chris had to take my pack off and carry it herself. Her only reason for doing this, let it be noted, was fear of ruining the contents. For my comfort she cared not a whit. I found this intimacy with the water monster exceedingly unpleasant, particularly as I could see no sense in this masochistic, fly-ridden torture whatsoever.

The swamp eventually ended, but we continued to follow the same watercourse for most of the day. We passed several small lakes; above each one, the river was noticeably smaller. By the time we made camp, it had shrunk to a stream no more than a couple of human paces across. We built our little fire on a rock right next to the spot where the shrunken river issued from a small, round, shallow lake. We were very close to the treeline; the mountainside that reared behind the lake was rugged and rocky, and most of it was covered by an unbroken blanket of snow. The wind blew and the rain splattered in fits and starts, but when I tried to seek shelter from the weather in a clump of subalpine fir, the mosquitos pounced onto my nose as if I were the first warm-blooded animal to come their way since creation. And indeed, we were now so far beyond any trace of human influence that were it not for the quite definite aroma of bear and moose, which animals the mosquitos no doubt also pursued, I might well have provided their first real feed of the year. By nightfall, my nose must have fed a cool million eggs for the next generation, and the sensitive skin around my eyes had become swollen and sore.

The wind gusted and beat all night, but the rain remained sporadic, and when our camp had been stuffed into our packs and we were ready to leave, golden bands of early-morning sun gleamed fitfully through the racing clouds. We crossed the little creek and climbed through the last vestiges of forest. We were soon plodding up the enormous snow patch, slithering a little on the slushy surface.

We had been protected from the wind somewhat on this northern face of the mountain, but as we reached the top, the gale hit us with a bang. "The Promised Land," Chris shouted into the wind.

Promised Land? I thought, aghast. She's finally done it. She's flipped.

All around was desolation. Tilted rock, swooping snow, a few scrubby patches of tundra and a vast sweep of sky arching toward a great wall of "dog-nosed mountains baying at the moon" (the quote, you may recall, is from that well-known writer Rabbit Service), all hung with veils of ice. I stared at Chris in some alarm. She was alight with a strange kind of fervour that I had never seen before. Was this, heaven forbid, going to be *it?*

But I am glad to say that "the promised land" was meant in a very broad sense only. It was what one might call a bit of artistic licence, a phrase I learned after Chris had acquired some success as a writer. Authors, apparently, are allowed to speak allegorically, and Chris was given to flights of rhetoric in her new-found status; I suppose she felt justified in using such a blatant exaggeration.

So on we went, but although we finally ended up at a spot below the treeline in a marginally kinder climate, I really wonder if it was a great deal better. The ground was rocky and harsh; the paucity of small animals gave testament to its bleakness; it was sparsely populated by trees that were monstrously distorted by great winds; the mosquitos thought it was Thanksgiving weekend; and, worst of all, the traces of human presence were so tenuous as to be almost non-existent. I had thought that Lonesome Lake represented the *ultima Thule* of civilization, but I was wrong; this was far, far worse.

And the following day, when the (by now) familiar waspish drone of an aircraft wavered into the still morning air, my last remaining hope that this was merely a temporary stop was destroyed. Out of the plane came those dreaded boxes, the tools and several bags of dog food. This, then, was where we were going to stay.

*And so we began, once more, the eternal round of
living in a camp. I was bored out of my mind.*

CHAPTER FOURTEEN

AND SO WE BEGAN, ONCE more, the eternal round of living in a camp: falling trees, peeling them, lugging them to the site and building a cabin. Chris had no help at all in this inhospitable place, and the logs had to be painstakingly dragged and lifted with ropes and a come-along. The bugs were terrible; the wind was maniacal; there were no neighbours anywhere near us—even the little visits across the river to pick up milk, as we had done at Lonesome Lake, were denied us here. Chris worked with dogged persistence; she was invariably exhausted and cranky at the end of the day, and I was once more bored out of my mind.

Chris called the place *Nuk Tessli*. That means "west wind" in the Carrier language; Chris named it after we were nearly blasted off the face of the earth by one of a series of gales that howled down the lake. Trees shrieked like souls demented and toppled like bowling pins. My fur was yanked in a million directions so that the very muscles at the roots became sore.

The government apparently frowned on the "simple" life in the bush, so Chris was obliged to come up with a commercial reason for our existence there. She decided, therefore, to create a small wilderness resort. She had the peculiar idea that other people might want to stay here and even pay money for the privilege. To this end, she started on a second cabin even before she had finished the first; the two buildings occupied the bulk of her time for three summers and the intervening winters.

The prospect of having visitors, paying guests or not, was at least something to look forward to, but—no surprise to me—few customers ever materialized. My only socializing occurred during the tree-planting seasons and the brief stays at Nimpo Lake, the tiny community that housed the float-plane company, when we walked out once a month to the post office. By this time, Chris had managed to have a few articles published in magazines, and she always scanned her mail anxiously for publishers' letters. She still wrote occasionally to the radio program. I rarely got a mention in any of these narrations, but there was one fearsome adventure that did earn me a modicum of fame. Needless to say, Chris's version of the incident (reported in her book *Diary of a Wilderness Dweller* and written about in one of her self-aggrandizing letters to the radio) differs a bit from mine.

Chris was never in a good mood when she was using the chainsaw, and I could certainly empathize for I too hated that high-pitched, screaming machine. I needed no persuading to stay by the tent, but our camp was only a little way along the shore, and I was not spared the saw's agonized wail—or Chris's cursing and swearing when things did not go according to plan. I always hated it when Chris raised her voice; I was never sure that her rage wasn't somehow directed at me.

A hot spell at the end of July encouraged a great hatching of horseflies; the irritating insects buzzed around one's head like bees. These great galumphing monsters had no finesse at all. The other biting flies at least had the delicacy to use very fine drills to penetrate the skin and often had the kindness to ameliorate their intrusions by a small quantity of anaesthetic. But if the horseflies managed to land on unprotected skin, they plunged their massive mandibles into our flesh with all the delicacy of a pair of blunt chisels and left a great, hard, itching lump behind. Fortunately, most of my body was well protected, but they still managed to get me on the thin rim of hairless skin around the eyes and on the end of my nose. A human's glabrous body covering is, of course, not designed for any kind of protection at all. Chris wore clothes over most of her limbs, but these made her doubly irritated as she did not possess the mechanism of panting to help cool herself off. Besides, she was unable to work with her hands and face covered, so these portions of her body were exposed.

While she was sawing above her head and balancing precariously on a wobbly log, a horsefly bit her on the throat. I heard a tremendous roar of rage that sounded something like "Get the **** **** out of here!" I could stand it no longer. Living at Lonesome Lake was one thing; there, at least, our neighbours induced a breath of civilization to the place. But here there was nothing: no good place to sleep, no sheltered campsite. The bugs were much worse, and social life was non-existent. Chris's yelling was simply the last straw. Without a word, I got up from the patch of shade in which I was lying and headed straight for the road.

The route to the outside world that Chris favoured at the time (it has since been altered quite a bit) followed our river down for several miles, then crossed it before climbing up the valley side and over the pass where she had shouted "The Promised Land!" On the other side was the long hike down that valley to where she had parked the truck. Close to the place where we crossed the river was an old trap cabin. We occasionally camped either in or beside it when we could not make the whole hike in one day. A bear had broken into the cabin at various times, and when we had last gone through, it was to find that he had ripped the door open and made a terrible mess with the few scraps of food that the trapper had left.

Things had been knocked all over the place, and coffee cans were crushed and punctured like colanders. As I approached it on my escape from Nuk Tessli, I could smell the bear close by. To reach the cabin, I would have had to swim The Wet. Chris always forced me to do that when she was along, but it was something I hated almost as much as the bear. So it was an easy decision to stay on the west side of the river, which soon emptied into the lake, particularly as there was a much overgrown but obviously once well-used horse trail leading around it. The horse trail forded the river at the bottom of the lake, but the riverbed was rocky there, and I was able to leap from boulder to boulder and cross with no real problem.

The trail wandered around in swamps and wriggled under wind-falls (I could imagine Chris's awkward frame having lots of fun with those!), and after a very long time I reached some buildings. I could smell at once that one of them was occupied, with a dog as well as some people. But it was already dark, and although the dog woofed a time or two when I came close, he was shut inside, and I could not make my presence known to the humans. So I curled up in the woodshed, pretty hungry without any supper, but there were no fresh bear smells, and I was also very tired after my energetic day, so I slept fairly well, all things considered.

Not long after daylight, there was some activity in the cabin. First the dog rushed out—a very beautiful malamute—and after he had swaggered around and let me know he was not to be fooled with, then realized that I was no threat at all to his machismo, I explained my predicament as best I could. The dog (who was called Ookpik, which means Snowy Owl, because of his colour, but whose humans had named him Taku) said he'd see if he could scrounge up some breakfast for me, and he scratched at the door and asked to be let back inside. Soon a short, rather kindly looking man came out with a cup of coffee in his hand. I have always been a polite creature and never one to intrude on anyone's privacy, so I made no noise but simply waited near the edge of the cleared space in front of the cabin until I was noticed. The man gazed for quite a while across the river (which was very wide there, as it was entering another huge lake), and his expression when he finally noticed me was quite comical. His eyebrows flew up, his mouth dropped open, and the ends of his moustache twitched. "Where on earth did you come from?" he said. He looked carefully all over the surface of the water. "The nearest cabin's miles away across the lake, and I don't see any fishermen in my bay." He turned to the cabin. "Marie. Look what we've got out here. It's a strange dog. She looks just like that mutt they call Brew on those TV ads." At which a pretty, dark-haired woman came to the door, also much surprised, but smiling. Since I was so polite and friendly, I was soon made much of. Ookpik's intervention was hardly needed, for soon an enormous plate of food was put in front of me, and a bed was made for me out of some blankets on the porch.

Feeling content and still somewhat tired after my previous day's exertions, I was only half-listening to the conversation, but I gathered that this cabin was still a long way from any other human neighbours; the nearest inhabited a gaggle of summer cottages many water miles away, and my new friends assumed that that was where I must have come from. They had no idea that anyone might be up the river. They had a radio phone and called around to see if anyone had lost a dog called "Brew," but of course no one had, and there was nothing either I or Ookpik could do to explain the situation differently. I gave an occasional guilty thought to Chris; I wondered if she would be at all worried about me or even notice that I had gone. She had been paying very little attention to me recently, and here I was being wonderfully spoiled, so perhaps she didn't miss me at all. Serves her right if she does, I thought to myself. If she lived a normal life, this kind of thing would never have happened.

Heavy rain started soon after I arrived, and none of us did very much but stay well fed, warm and dry. After a couple of days of this idyllic existence (when, I must confess, I was just beginning to wonder about Chris a little. After all, I thought, she did care for me in her own human manner, and I was even beginning to miss her crankiness, strange as that may seem), a boat came puttering through the rain and tied up at our dock. (There was a plane tied at the dock as well. It belonged to Ookpik's family.) The man, Ookpik and I all trotted out to greet the newcomers, and at once I knew that some pretty drastic diplomacy was called for. Under normal circumstances, with a stranger, I would simply have waited to be noticed, but in this instance I increased my pace to a run and without a pause leapt straight into the boat. This was the last place I would normally have chosen to be, for even being on top of The Wet was scary enough, but in the boat, beside a youth who was holding onto the tiller, both of them looking very wet and bedraggled, was Chris.

I decided an abject apology would be carrying things too far— after all, it was Chris's fault I was here in the first place—but did not want to incur too much wrath by not looking contrite at all. In the end I settled for an "I-knew-you'd-find-me-sooner-or-later" expression, and it seemed to work. In any case, although I could see that Chris was pretty angry, I knew full well that she wouldn't let her real feelings run rampant in front of all these other humans. She explained to my new friends how she had gone out to Nimpo over the usual route—in dumping rain that had washed away any tracks I might have made—expecting me to have tried to find the truck or gone out to the settlement that straggled around the float-plane base. Chris did the rounds of the resorts and asked everyone if they had any news of a lost dog. One of the float-plane companies had heard the query from Ookpik's humans' radio phone, and that was how Chris had found me. There being no road to this place, she had begged a ride in a boat from some people living 12 miles away at the other end of the lake.

And what, might you think, was particularly fearsome about that adventure? Well, just bear with me; the really scary bit hasn't happened yet.

Chris decided that she needed some stuff from Williams Lake, so we spent a couple of days shopping and then a couple more days on the trail going home while Chris brushed out the thick section of forest just above the trap cabin. Thus it was four days after we had left Ookpik and his family that we arrived at this rough shelter. It was close to dark, so Chris elected to stay the night, even though I tried to persuade her not to, for the fresh bear smell was very strong. I found it absolutely amazing that Chris could not register the aroma herself, or if she did, that she would ignore such a strong message to keep away.

But she unloaded our packs, spread her bed roll on the wood-chip floor, cooked herself some supper on the warped tin stove, crawled into her sleeping bag, propped herself up against the wall and opened one of the cabin's paperbacks on her chest, with a candle balanced in front of her chin for light. The small windows of the cabin had been nailed shut in an abortive attempt to keep the bear out, and she left the door open so that she would know when daylight was coming. She wanted to be up and away early in the morning.

In fact, it was not the daylight but I who woke her. I barked with all the ferocity that I could muster. The bear was right beside the cabin.

At Stuie, when I was with Tan Sister, we had often chased bears, tearing after them and barking our heads off to great effect. But, as I have already mentioned, when I was alone and tried the same tactics, the bears always took one look at me and either ignored me completely or came after me instead. And now, even though I barked myself silly, this bear, a big black boar, simply kept coming. Contrary to popular belief, black bears can be just as dangerous as grizzlies; they enjoy a tasty puppy dog for supper and will sometimes even hunt humans for food. This one was in a foul mood, snarling and laying back his ears in anger. Now, I had encountered hundreds of bears by that point, and many had given me a good fright, but I'd never before seen one that was really angry. I was absolutely petrified. Chris could have all the wilderness she wanted—but she could have it without me.

Off I ran to the nearest friend I knew: Ookpik, at the mouth of the river. It was a trip, I heard Chris say later, that would have taken her at least a whole day, but four legs work a lot better than two; the bear had attacked us just as the first light was creeping into the sky, and I arrived at the cabin at the mouth of the river when the man was having his breakfast.

But instead of making a lot of fuss over me as he had done before, he gently but quite firmly put me into the plane that was tied up against his wharf. Here was another terror thrown at me; I simply could not imagine what was going to happen. The tremendous roar of the motor and the fight with the water monster that I had now observed so often ensued, but this time, I was in the very belly of the flying truck. And then, unbelievably, we were wobbling over the river I had just run along; within minutes we swooshed to a landing on Chris's lake. The man taxied to Chris's crude log wharf and left me at the tent. She wasn't there, of course; I knew very well where she would be—if the bear had not eaten her up altogether—and tried to tell the man, but to no avail. In this day and age of technological advances in so many directions, we still have a long way to go in the field of basic communication.

I'm not sure what I would have done if Chris had not also appeared right then. She was still over on the other side of the lake, and the man had already flung his plane into the air. But as he turned to fly back home, he saw Chris begin to steer her canoe across the water. He landed again and taxied right up to the boat. The two voices came to me plainly, and I heard how Chris had thought the bear's crunching footsteps in the debris around the cabin were mine! She had actually said, "Good girl, Lonesome" at the moment the bear stuck his head into the window. She herself got a terrible fright this time but was able to drive the bear off by whacking an axe against an oil drum and making a lot of noise, even though the bear actually charged her. Once it left, she threw her equipment together, waded across the river and walked as fast as possible toward her camp, calling me as she went, but convinced I was no more. I had left her nearly three hours earlier, and it had taken her all this time to walk up the river. The man with the flying truck of course knew nothing of all this drama and had assumed I had merely "run off again," as he rather unkindly phrased it. If he only knew what I had to put up with, he might have been more sympathetic.

Well, Chris was pretty delighted to see me this time, and she made a great fuss. But I received a terrible punishment: I was tied up at the camp all day like a puppy for some time afterward. I've always hated being on a lead, and this time I could not help but think of the rabbits wearing the golden wire collars at Miner Lake. Nothing like that happened to me, of course, but such an indignity was still a dreadful disgrace.

When we were first reunited, Chris was delighted at my response to her, which was quite agitated with a lot of whining and bum-waggling and the like. Her typical human ego translated it into the idea that I was so thrilled to see her safe. Which I was, of course, but I was actually trying to tell her about the plane. From the lakeshore, the whole business of fighting with the water monster to get one up into the air looks pretty horrifying. —*But just think*, I tried to tell her, —*how quickly and easily we can travel over that rough and very dangerous country. Why can't we have a plane as well?*

She didn't listen, of course. But dogs have to accept that humans are illogical creatures, and they must simply expect these trouble-some idiosyncrasies as part of their lot.

CHAPTER FIFTEEN

NIMPO LAKE WAS NOW OUR link with the outside world. The main street boasted a grand total of three buildings: a motel, a store with a gas pump, and a restaurant that also housed the post office. These would not have existed at all were it not for the lake's reputation as a fishing area—humans play with fish in much the same way we dogs chase squeakers. The small core of permanent residents and their families who ran the resorts, float-plane companies and other businesses could not have amounted to more than 50 souls.

However, a short distance away was the much larger (three stores, no less!) community of Anahim Lake. This did duty as the administrative centre for the vast, sparsely inhabited area that enclosed the two communities. As well as the stores, Anahim boasted an Indian reserve, a couple of garages, a medical clinic, an RCMP detachment, another restaurant and a second motel, several more resorts and a school. It was also, like Bella Coola, a community of dogs. I have mentioned all this in some detail because it was here that we met Sport, who was eventually to become the third member of our pack.

The hike to the road, even after Chris had made a much easier trail through the forest, was never anything less than an expedition. Different routes had to be taken when weather conditions changed, but no matter which way we went, there were inevitable confrontations with storms, brush, flies and the water monster. Rivers or parts

The hike to the road was never anything less than an expedition.

of lakes had to be swum, forded, tentatively tiptoed across when frozen, or balanced above on conveniently fallen trees—although these last were precarious at best, for even if it couldn't engulf the logs, the water monster usually managed to spit all over them and render them slippery in the extreme. The summer hike to the road often involved spending at least one night in a camp (invariably redolent with bear), and the winter trips were route marches of great magnitude involving two to three days of slogging through unbroken snow, topped by a final day on snow-machine trails, before we reached the blessed security of the scrap of civilization Chris now called town.

Once out there, Chris often found it necessary to go to the school, as it boasted the community's photocopying machine. And the school (when it was in session) was the principal hangout for the community's dogs. Even in the most miserable winter weather they would be found in shivering groups on the doorstep, waiting for recess, when they would avidly consume whatever lunches the kids chose to discard, either directly into their eager jaws or indirectly via the garbage cans. These dogs, as you can imagine, came in colours, shapes and sizes that sometimes defied description; I well remember a wiry-haired, brown-and-white, stumpy-limbed individual whose body was as long as mine but whose legs were so short he could barely clear the steps. This unfortunate creature had managed to get into the garbage can that squatted by the back door, but he couldn't get out. Chris happened to walk by and hear his appeal for help, and although she laughed to see him in his predicament, she was kind enough to fish him out and set him on his way. He was absolutely plastered with ketchup and mayonnaise (it was Hamburger Day at school), and a couple of fetching bits of lettuce sat rakishly over his ears. Needless to say,

I took no part at all in this disgraceful display of licentiousness, but merely stayed in the truck box and disassociated myself from the whole spectacle as best I could. Occasionally I needed to curl a lip at some ill-mannered lout who was bold enough to rear against the side of the truck box and poke his nose over the top, but I am glad to say that even the most dimwitted soon learned to leave me alone.

Sport was not actually part of this undisciplined mob, but it was through the school that we met him. If Chris had a lot of copying to do, she would go there after the students had left for the day, and she consequently became friends with the janitor. The janitor was looking for a new home for her dog, Sport. Sport was basically a Lab-shepherd cross and therefore of a good size; he was of an amiable disposition, and he was three years old.

"He was the kids' dog, really, and now they're away from home so much, he's just an extra mouth to feed. We like our dogs to bark when people come, because we have a lot of expensive ranching machinery in the yard, and Sport is too friendly for that. He just wags his tail."

"That's the kind of dog I need," said Chris. "I can't stand a dog that barks all the time. And if I'm going to start a tourist business, I want an animal that's friendly with everyone, especially kids. But I don't want anything that chases wildlife. Lonesome is so good about that." (Praise such as this was rare indeed!)

"Well," said the woman carefully, "he does chase squirrels sometimes."

"Oh well, I guess that's fairly normal. The other problem is that I'm flying home in a couple of days, as the conditions for snowshoeing are terrible right now. Is he used to vehicles?"

"Actually, we've never had him in a car."

"Hmm. Well, I guess he's used to being tied."

"I'm afraid not. He's never needed to be tied. He doesn't even wear a collar."

"Oh dear. I guess I'd better put a string on him and drive him around in the truck for a while and see how he does."

So we went around to the house, which was in the bush a little way out of Anahim, and were greeted by two ferociously barking dogs and a third who had the general shape and colour of a golden Lab, but was larger and chunkier and bore on his sides the dark shadows of his Teutonic parentage. He was rather retiring and quite polite, but I could see at once that he was simple-minded. He couldn't even remember his real name; Sport was the only title to which he ever aspired.

Chris talked to him, and he allowed her to slip a string around his neck and lead him around in a circle. He didn't particularly like this (and I fully sympathized with him there), but he followed well enough. Then Chris opened the passenger door of the truck and cajoled him inside. He whimpered a little and looked alarmed, but made very little protest. Chris drove around the block, and I could see through the glass back of the cab that he looked very nervous, but he remained otherwise docile. The upshot of this was that Chris decided to take him with us.

I had, as you can imagine, become very pleased indeed when I heard that Chris had started to come to her senses and decided to forego some of the worst winter slogs in and out of Nuk Tessli. I have loved flying from the moment I first got into Ookpik's plane, but Chris is a veritable basket case; she has a flying phobia that nothing has so far been able to cure. And Sport, it turned out, was quite a wimp as far as any vehicle was concerned.

—*Relax!* I tried to tell them as I hopped happily into the

aircraft. —*You'll only be in the air for 20 minutes. Think of all that misery of snow and Wet that we'll avoid.* But neither Chris nor Sport could be consoled, and they were both as jittery as deer mice until we landed on the ice beside the cabins.

The three of us had taken up a good portion of the aircraft, and as there were a lot of supplies to come in, a second flight had to be chartered. Thus there was an enormous pile of freight to haul up off the lake. Chris trotted back and forth on her snowshoes, pulling the toboggan and talking to Sport quite a bit (and ignoring me entirely; I curled up in my little kennel on the porch and disregarded her in return). Slowly she stashed away all the bags and packages of dog and human food and her books, clothes, art supplies, tools, correspondence and other bric-a-brac with which she deems it necessary to surround herself.

All of a sudden, I heard her voice rise in a panic.

"Sport! Sport!"

He had disappeared. Chris abandoned the toboggan, cast around for footprints and set off as fast as possible in pursuit. The snow was deep and soft on the lake, with an inch or so of water between the snow and the ice, and she could not make very quick progress—and in conditions like that, I never set foot on the lake if I can help it, as I sink right into the water layer and get my feet wet. So I waited back at the cabin and watched Chris as she struggled around one of the islands on the lake. Sport had travelled about half a mile and was just about to enter the bush. He must have heard Chris calling, but it was only when he saw her that he ran back. I tried to tell Chris that he really wasn't worth the bother, that it would have been better just to let him go, but Chris praised him mightily for returning to her and spoke in some amazement of the fact that he had been heading straight for his former home. (—*And where else might he have gone?* I asked.) Although she tied him up after that, she lavished gooey compliments upon him in the degrading and embarrassing way that many humans speak to their canines, and which she (thank Dog!) never did to me. Sport responded by whining and whimpering and generally behaving like a spoiled puppy. As a result of which, all Chris did was speak sympathetically to him! If I had wailed and complained in such a way, I would have received very short shrift, let me tell you.

Humans' lack of perspicacity never ceases to amaze me. That Chris couldn't see Sport's real concerns! It wasn't his pack he was pining for. It was his food dish. I tried to tell him that supper would be coming eventually, but he was so stupid he simply didn't believe me. It was not until a wash basin full of kibble was placed in front of him that he finally understood. With a grin of incredulous delight, he promptly flopped down on his stomach, spread his front legs on either side of the dish and commenced to guzzle. As soon as he discovered that food was regularly forthcoming, he never attempted to leave Chris again.

Despite Sport's eventual usefulness as a pack dog, he had several irritating habits, not the least of which was his impolite method of dealing with his meals. In eating as in everything else, I conducted myself with gentility and decorum, but Sport had obviously received no training in basic manners, or if he had, he was simply too stupid to assimilate it. He ate every single chunk of kibble individually, chomping each one with slavering gusto, until any listener was driven mad by the monotonous, rhythmic **CRUNCH crunch crunch** crunch crunch; **CRUNCH crunch crunch** crunch crunch; **CRUNCH crunch crunch** crunch crunch.

Moreover, his plebeian attitudes to food were lamentable. Labs apparently are prone to this. When we stayed at Nimpo Lake, he would head for the nearest garbage can, or even hike right over to the dump. Tying him up was not a complete solution, for he whimpered and whined, and the second Chris was out of sight, he yodelled like a coloratura soprano. But the moment he was set loose, he was gone. When chastised, he never even had the grace to look ashamed. (I must confess to being a little envious of this blatant lack of respect for Chris's wishes at these times. The aromas that clung to his coat after these expeditions were often delightful.)

Chris learned of Sport's propensity for gluttony a day or two after we first flew in to Nuk Tessli. The steps to the attic were in the porch area, right by the two dog kennels, and Chris was in the habit of leaving items on them ready to take upstairs the next time she was heading that way. I, of course, was far too well bred to touch anything, but Sport had no such inhibitions. Imagine Chris's ire to find him with his head stuck happily in a honey bucket. No saccharine endearments then! And Sport's only reaction was total bewilderment as to why anyone should speak harshly to him.

We stayed at Nuk Tessli for three months that winter, after which it was time to go tree planting again. Travelling conditions had improved considerably—the snow was firmer and the days were longer—so we were going to go back out to Nimpo on foot. That hike was to be Sport's first major trip—and the first time he would carry a serious load.

Chris had learned from her experiences with me (didn't I tell you she was smarter than most humans?), and she did not expect him to start backpacking cold. During our winter snowshoe tramps, she had frequently put a set of saddlebags on his back, empty at first, and later padded out with coats and suchlike to give bulk. But I am afraid that although he was never really bothered by the pack itself, Sport consistently failed to understand that he was wider than normal when carrying it. When he connected with a rock or tree, it was the rock or tree, as far as he was concerned, that would have to move. He could trash a backpack in a season, whereas my pack, although it had accumulated a few patches after several years' hard wear, was the same one I had used from the beginning.

These trips out at the start of the tree-planting season were often the best of the year. The route we would have used if we had gone out earlier in the winter ran down the river all the way to Ookpik's house, then across the ice of the huge lake where we parked the truck in summer, connecting finally with snow-machine trails along the logging roads. But in April, the ice started to go at lower elevations, and that route became a miserable hodgepodge of sludgy snow, windfall and swamp. Rivers had to be waded, and the lake ice was often suspect, so all the lakes had to be laboriously circumnavigated. The snow above the treeline, however, was usually firm at that time of year, and its smooth, windblown cover enabled us to run over areas that would be covered in dense tangles of brush or tilted rock slides in summer.

Sport, of course, was aware of none of this. When Chris put his pack on him (bulging quite gratifyingly, I was pleased to see), he whimpered a little at the unaccustomed weight, but obviously assumed that we were simply going on one of our usual walks and he would be back at his food dish in good time for supper. I made no effort to disillusion the poor sop—he would find out what it was all about soon enough.

To climb up to the alpine area, one must first rise steeply up the ridge that encloses the southern edge of the lake. Sport and I were packing as usual, but Chris pulled items that would not fit into our bags on a little plastic toboggan. She arranged her load so that the straps of her backpack were uppermost; when the way was steep, she was able to lift the whole thing, toboggan and all, onto her back.

—*Dog*, grinned Sport delightedly. —*She looks like a cross between a crazy beetle and a heron, with those long legs sticking out the back. Doesn't she have any idea how funny she looks?*

I was quite shocked at his blatant vulgarity. —*You have to remember that a human's physique has distinctive limitations*, I admonished him primly. Privately, though, I considered the analogy a remarkably good one and was a little piqued that I had not thought of it myself.

At the top of the first steep climb, the ground flattened. We headed straight into the low rays of the morning sun as it lanced through the trees. The going was easy, for the snow was firm, and the two lakes we subsequently traversed were solidly iced and as comfortable to walk on as a sidewalk. Then ensued a long, slow climb to the treeline. The scrubby pines grew sparser and finally dropped away until we were on a high plateau that I knew would be running with creeks and full of flowers in summer, but which was now so smoothly paved with crusted snow that we were able to walk upon it without sinking. As the sun arched higher, we crested a height of land and dropped slightly again, trotting easily through a high valley. We used the ice of its small lakes as a roadway until the highest part of the journey, Halfway Mountain, was before us.

Up to this point, Sport had been enjoying himself fairly well. Through the forested areas he had bounded enthusiastically after squirrels, crashing his saddlebags with supreme indifference into every obstacle that presented itself and generally behaving in his usual gauche manner, much like a young human at the prospect of getting out of school. He had, however, never carried a pack either as heavy as this or for as long a period of time; indeed, he had never walked as far as this in his life (a few runs after a snow machine in winter had been his total ration of exercise during the first three years of his existence). I had long since learned to pace myself and, like Chris, was steadily plodding along at the same speed with which we had begun. The weather was good, although the sun was a little too hot and the surface of the snow had begun to soften. Soon Sport was dragging both his head and his heels and whining a little to himself under his breath.

—*What's the point of all this? I'm hungry. There are no squirrels here. I want to go home. Isn't it suppertime yet?* And so on.

—*Shape up, for goodness' sake*, I hissed, but to no avail.

At the foot of Halfway Mountain, the summer and winter routes diverged. The summer route runs around the north side of the mountain, but it traverses a steep slope, and the snow often avalanches down it in winter. Around the south of the mountain is an old horse trail that has a much friendlier grade and therefore is ideal in winter, but whose swamps make it unpleasant in summer. Of course there is no sign of the horse trail under six or eight feet of snow, and in looking for the route, Chris made a mistake. We should have continued to drop toward one of the many lakes that dot the valley, but in an effort to forego this loss of altitude, Chris tried to maintain an even height. We soon ran into difficulties. A steep-sided ridge, mostly blown bare of snow, blocked our way. The sensible solution would have been to slither down into the valley bottom, where we should have been in the first place, and climb back up on the other side of the ridge. But Chris was not getting any younger (we had both entered our middle years at approximately the same time), and the thought of losing her hard-won altitude was not one she wanted to contemplate.

She eyed the mountain above us. The steep rock slide, stripped clean by sun and wind, soared above us. "It doesn't look too bad, does it, Lonesome?" she said. "If we go up here we should be able to cut across to the pass we want without any problem and save ourselves quite a trek out of our way."

—*Now come along, Chris*, I admonished with a lift of my eyebrow. —*You know very well that every time you take shortcuts they're always worse than they initially appear. You've got us into trouble with that attitude many a time.* But of course she did not listen to me.

Sport was either oblivious to this exchange or ignorant of its portent, for he remained in his private dudgeon, muttering his complaints. (He was not at all good at languages, and the only human words he ever bothered to learn were his name and *supper*, *dinner*, *kibble*, *cookie*, *treat* and the like.) But when Chris began to scramble laboriously up the boulders, the blue toboggan hoisted on her back, holding her snowshoes in her hands and digging their tails into the scree for support, Sport turned to me aghast.

—*What's she doing now, for Dog's sake? Is she crazy or what?* And then: —*Hey, don't leave me! Wait! Waaaaaiiiiit!* And his voice rose dramatically into a long, protesting howl.

Chris turned toward him in astonishment.

"Sport! What a racket! Come on, you big baby! Come on!"

I, of course, was quietly picking my way in her wake, saving my breath for the climb.

Sport put a foot on a rock; it slipped. He heaved himself up with a jump, but the weight of his pack pulled him back. He scrambled awkwardly onto another boulder, the pack crashed against a stone, and he was knocked down again.

—*Owwowwowwwwowwwoww!* he cried. But Chris, though she gave him a glance occasionally to make sure he was not in any real difficulty, simply forged on ahead and let him work it out for himself. And with pitiful wails and moans every step of the way, he began to climb.

My predictions regarding the "shortcut" were, needless to say, quite correct. The higher we got, the steeper and more difficult the rock slide became. It swooped dizzily down to the icy slope at its foot; Chris soon had the familiar pinched-mouth look of heartily wishing she was somewhere else. The slope got so precipitous in the end that she had to take off our packs and let us scramble up unencumbered. She would heave the packs to a ledge over her head, haul herself up and toss our packs up the next step. All three of us were mightily glad to reach the top.

But our troubles were not yet over. Far from being an easy route to the pass, our way in that direction was barred by a formidable wall of rock and ice.

"****," said Chris.

—*I told you so*, I panted, beginning to shiver in the keen wind that hit us now that we were more exposed.

"Well, I'm not going back down there again. It looks like the only route from here is to go right over the top of the mountain and cross it by that high saddle between the peaks."

So that is what we did.

It was a long slog up to the saddle, not difficult, but uncomfortable in the extreme, for the wind howled bitterly up there.

Parts of the slope were blown bare, and parts were covered with a fine, silty snow into which Chris sank knee deep. It was a question of either putting on and taking off the snowshoes every five minutes, or ploughing through the snow patches in boots alone. We dogs, of course, had no choice.

Finally we gained the highest point of the saddle. The wind had reached maniacal proportions, and I fully expected that we would scurry down the leeward side of the mountain to get away from its bite as quickly as possible. But not a bit of it. Chris shouted with joy and at once flung off her pack and fished for her camera.

"You guys are going to have to pose for me," she bellowed into the teeth of the wind. "Just look at those mountains! And you can see my lake down there. It looks like complete wilderness. There's no sign of any human presence at all from this altitude. No, stay, Lonesome. Sport, STAY!" But of course, he wouldn't. In the end, Chris crossly tied him to her pack, and she made me lie down beside him. Quickly she backed off and took her snap, but I have never liked that cyclopean eye pointed at me, and Sport was looking so confused and miserable, hunching himself over as if he had been whipped, that we can't have made a very satisfactory grouping. Humans' mania for optical stimulation is hard to understand. Why standing on a barren outcrop in bitter winds in the middle of winter should be cause for such elation is baffling in the extreme.

Sport had dense under-fur and was less affected by the wind than I was. My genetic heritage had ill equipped me for arctic climes, and the fine powdery ice would always be driven right against my skin. But in the lee of the saddle, we soon received our promised shelter. At first the downward slope was gentle, but the gradient rapidly became steep again. Chris crept along, trying to kick steps into its icy surface with her soft-soled snowpacs (it was too steep and slippery for the snowshoes). We dogs fared a little better here, as our claws gave us some purchase. Finally we reached the solace of flatter ground. At that point, however, we entered the forest, and at once the snow was as soft as warm butter. Chris sank to her thighs, even with snowshoes on, and we dogs floundered behind.

Despite his heavy load, Sport negotiated these conditions with comparatively little effort, as he was blessed with long legs and large feet. Even using his tracks, my dainty paws sank farther, and my belly became clogged with icy balls of snow. I put on my most martyred expression, hoping Chris would take note of the extent of my sacrifice for her, but she was groaning and sighing almost as badly as Sport at this stage. However, it wasn't long before even she decided that this kind of torture was a waste of effort, and she found a densely overhanging spruce under which to make camp.

We had been following a little creek for a while; most of it was still buried in snow, but an open hole allowed us access to water, and we were all very glad to take a rest. Chris lit her usual cooking fire, and I crouched beside it as closely as I could with my paws stretched to the flames. For a few hours, at least, we were comfortable.

The following morning the surface of the snow froze sufficiently to enable us to finish our descent through the trees with slightly more facility, and once we had crossed the creek at the bottom and reconnected with the summer trail, the going was not too bad.

There was only one instance of note on that latter part of the

I put on my most martyred expression, hoping Chris would take note and make camp.

trip. Some years at this time, the lower lakes that dot this river are open. But that winter had seen a heavy snowpack, and as a result, some of the ice on the lakes was intact. Travel on the ice was much faster than on land, but we had to use the ice carefully, for those lakes were known to be tricky. Chris progressed with extreme caution, using only the safest-looking inlets, whacking the axe periodically on the surface in front of her to test the texture and thickness of the ice.

Sport had recovered his equanimity considerably on the second day (after he realized that his kibble had travelled with him), and he trotted along the ice without protest. He had been presented with a considerable number of backpacking experiences on this trip, but there was one lesson he had yet to learn.

We dogs love to roll on hard-frozen snow. It is the only manifestation of the water monster that I can come even close to enjoying. And Sport, presented with this cold, flat surface, instinctively put his shoulder down to roll.

—*You'll regret it*, I warned him. But nobody ever takes any notice of me. Well, he got onto his back all right, but his packs held him down, and try as he might he could not get up on his feet again. His legs paddled uselessly in the air like those of a discombobulated beetle, and his expression of bewilderment was so comical that even Chris was able to recognize it, and she roared with laughter. Now, Sport might be simple-minded, but he didn't really deserve such unwarranted mirth. He was only a beginner, after all. Needless to say, Chris did not leave him in difficulties for long, and she righted him with a yank and a chuckle. And oddly enough, it was the one lesson he actually learned. Sometimes he forgot himself so far as to begin his roll, but as soon as one of his bags touched the ground, he would remember and quit.

Sport never did his job with much finesse, and I would certainly have preferred a more intellectual companion, but he was a strong dog and ended up doing a great deal of heavy work. So I had to admit that he had his uses. Perhaps if he'd had more brains he would have balked at some of the tasks set before us, but despite his litany of complaints, it could probably be said that he earned his kibble. It certainly did Chris and me no harm to have a bit of mindless male muscle around some of the time.

Sport never did his job with much finesse, but I had to admit that he had his uses.

CHAPTER SIXTEEN

SPORT HAD A CHARACTERISTIC THAT set him apart from other dogs. Although he rarely barked, his other vocal accomplishments were extraordinary. His virtuoso performances extracted gasps of wonder and amazement from any human who heard them. When presented with an obstacle that he felt was beyond his capabilities, he would ululate a piercing, flute-like warble in a pitch that covered at least two octaves and wavered somewhere between a soprano and a contralto. Its purity of tone would have been the envy of any castrato. (Which, of course, he was.)

Like me, he hated water. After tree-planting season, we usually returned to Nuk Tessli in late June or early July, and at that time of year most of the streams and creeks were in full flood. Several watercourses had to be waded, and any of the alpine country not covered in snow was sodden and running with meltwater. Chris loved this time of year, for even under several inches of icy liquid, the first urgent spring flowers were already in bloom. These scentless, bland shapes excite some humans greatly. As far as I was concerned, this time of year was something of a trial. Chris's legs were wet only from the ankles down, and even Sport was able to hop over most of the unpleasantness, but for me it was sheer misery. The water monster roared and chuckled in every direction; The Wet itself was no warmer than the ice from which it issued, and my fur was constantly soaked to the skin.

Three creeks, at that time of year, needed a little planning to cross. One, if we were lucky, would still be snowbridged; otherwise Chris would have to wade, and Sport and I would have to cross by a mixture of rock-leaping and swimming. (Chris always had the presence of mind to remove our packs and carry them herself at these times. At first I used to think that this largesse was a gratifying concern for our welfare; afterward I came to realize that she simply wanted to keep her possessions dry.)

And then, of course, there was the river. During high water, it was enormously difficult to cross. Chris had made several attempts to find routes over it, and at the time of Sport's first spring trip home, we had to swim a stretch that was as wide as a six-lane freeway. Chris chose this area because it was one of the few sections of the river where the water monster was comparatively placid and did not show its teeth.

Sport had given voice to his usual assemblage of moans and whimpers, but it was not until we reached the bigger stretch of water that he really gave tongue. —*Owowowowowoooooooooo*, he sang, although Sport was, in fact, a very strong swimmer. —*Owowowowowooooooooow!* His feet churned like paddles, and his powerful shoulders pulled him through the water at twice the speed I could manage. I simply concentrated on swimming and saving my breath.

But it was when we came to Chris's lake that Sport gave his best performance. During the winter, Chris had dragged her canoe across the ice so that it would be ready for her when she reached our lake in spring. Otherwise, we would have been faced with a long, swampy slog and another river crossing before we could reach the cabin. I say "we," you'll notice; on previous occasions, she had always let me ride in the canoe with her. But this time, she did things a little differently.

During high water, the river was enormously difficult to cross, and
we had to swim a stretch that was as wide as a six-lane freeway.

"You've got to stay with Sport, Lonesome," Chris said. "He's only been here in the winter, and he doesn't know the trail home around the lake. You'll have to show him where to go."

Needless to say, I was far from happy about this. I was just as tired and leg-weary as Chris. But my human took no notice of my doleful expression; she merely loaded all three packs into the canoe, hopped in behind them and commenced to paddle.

—*Owowowowowowooooooow!* said Sport loudly at once.

"For goodness' sake, Sport, shut up."

—*OWOWOWOWOWOWOWOWOOOOOOOOW!*

—*Sport!* I hissed with a curl of my lip. —*She's only going to canoe along the shore. All we have to do is run alongside.*

—*Wooooooooow*, he moaned. —*Wowooooovnooow*. But he did finally cotton on to a certain degree and began to follow me, keeping his eyes, however, on the canoe. At every little jutting point along the shore, he ran to its very tip and warbled.

"SHUT UP, SPORT," yelled Chris. I could see that she was getting cross. But he simply would not stop.

In windy weather, Chris would continue all the way round the back of the lake, crossing it behind one of the numerous islands that dotted its northeast end. But when the water was calm, as it was on this occasion, she would paddle to a point almost opposite the cabin, then head straight over. The distance across was about three-quarters of a mile. I began to wonder, with no little trepidation, what was in store for me that day. Chris had never made me swim such a distance before. But to my relief, she nosed the canoe into the bank and called me to jump in (which I could now do with great dexterity). Sport immediately ran up and put a paw on the gunwale.

"No!" Chris yelled, and pushed at him with the paddle.

—*Wooooooow*, said Sport, not understanding what was happening, but ready to complain as a matter of formality.

—*You can do one of two things*, I told him, swaying easily to the small lift of the boat. —*You can either run along the shore round the back of the lake or swim after us.*

—*Wooooooowowowowowo. Don't gowowowowowowowo!*

"Come on, Sport," said Chris cajolingly in her come-to-supper voice (although the undercurrent of irritation was not entirely disguised). "Come on . . . good boy."

—*WOWOWOWOWOWOWOWOWO! Why can't I come in with youwouwouw?*

—*Because you've never been in a boat before and you might tip it over*, I explained patiently. —*This isn't like a truck, you know. It takes skill to be a good passenger in one of these. You're a great big strong dog. You can do it easily.*

—*OWOWOWOWOWOWOWOWOWOWOOOW!* And in he plunged.

Chris stayed beside him, canoeing slowly and calling to him. And indeed, he made the crossing with no trouble at all. Three-quarters of the way over, he scrambled onto an island only to find himself with another gulf of water widening between us.

—*OWOWOWOWO*, he yodelled piteously.

—*Sport*, I stated firmly. —*This is really embarrassing. Chris won't like it at all. She hates noise. Shape up like a dog. What's wrong with you?*

—*It's all right for youwouwouwouwou*, he wailed. —*You're in the bowowowowowoat.*

—*You would be too if you didn't struggle and pace about so much in a vehicle. You'd have to be tied in here or you'd just try and jump out. Pull yourself together!*

—But it's COWOWOWOWOWOWOWOWOOOOOOLD!

And in he leapt again. Sport's howling at being confronted with a body of water was a habit that neither Chris nor I was ever to break. In all the years that he lived with us, he never once let Chris enjoy a pristine morning's canoeing. Even when he knew the trails well, Sport would howl and moan and whimper every inch of the way.

CHAPTER SEVENTEEN

JUST OVER A YEAR AFTER Sport came to live with us, Chris went to work for a different tree-planting company. This crew planted on the coast as well as in the Interior, and due to the peculiarities of British Columbia's mild coastal climate, work could start at the end of February.

We were to meet the crew at the north end of Vancouver Island. The site was only about 150 miles from Nuk Tessli as the float plane flies, but to get there we had to drive all the way east to Williams Lake, south and west to Vancouver Island, and back up north to the little logging town of Woss. Chris checked at the single restaurant-cum-store-cum-PO-cum-gas-station and found, among the faded scraps of paper advertising community affairs, the expected barely legible scribble that directed her to the tree-planters' camp. We went back onto the highway for another 14 klicks, then turned off at a flagging-tape arrow, bumped along a bush road and found ourselves in a wide, bare space that had originally been cleared for a gold mine. At one end, the boarded-up entrance and the bulked, rusted remains of some of the machinery had partially succumbed to the encroaching forest. At the other end was a small lake. Everything smelled wet and green and earthy. It had been 40 below on the day we had driven out of Nimpo Lake; at Woss camp, it was raining.

Although the crew was new to Chris, the straggle of tents and beat-up campers clustered around a large, plastic-walled, tarp-roofed cookshack was familiar enough. There was the usual potpourri of smells: cookies and soup; the chemicals sprayed on the seedlings; filthy, sweat-soaked clothes mouldering in the shower tent; and the individual aromas of a number of individuals, most of whom were out of camp at that moment. But all of this was wiped instantly from my mind, for as the truck ground to a halt, we were greeted by an absolute bedlam of barking, and a huge phalanx of ferocious dogs tore in a mass to meet us.

Even Chris was a little perturbed at the manner of our reception. There were seven great beasts all told, the leader of whom was ferocious in the extreme. He was, more or less, a Bouvier; his coat was a ragged mat of black dreadlocks (a hairstyle much in fashion in camp at the time), and his canines protruded from his jaw like Dracula fangs.

To say that I was appalled was an understatement. Sport and I both cowered in the truck box, and Chris sat for a moment before cautiously opening her door and warily extending a leg into the melee. But she was, compared with most humans, a moderately good student of dogspeak (thanks to my patient coaching, I might add), and, finding that the barks and ferocious slaverings did not extend to growling (except from an old St. Bernard cross who delivered a stream of invective that could have taught my human a thing or two had she but understood, but who, fortunately, stayed by her camper), Chris waded through the throng and followed her nose to the kitchen. The volume of noise that issued from this humble edifice was as loud as the combined efforts of the dogs—the Grateful Dead, if my memory serves me correctly—and Chris entered it with her fingers stuffed into her ears. The tape shut off abruptly, and the usual shrill human bleats of greetings were exchanged.

Meanwhile, Sport and I were coping with the ring of red-mawed, dripping-tongued visages that had reared against the side of the truck. I had to lift my teeth a little at the advances of one large young animal, who proved to be the son of the cranky old bitch by the camper, but his forwardness was due only to his immaturity, and he backed off readily enough.

For the rest, they were a motley bunch, their only relationship being their size; every single one was bigger even than Sport, which made their proportions quite formidable. I had never seen so many dogs in a tree-planting camp before.

One animal stood out from the rest. Apart from the crabby old grandmother still bellowing and snarling beside her human's camper, she was the only female in the pack. She was very beautiful: mostly malamute, but with a long, sweeping silvery coat that looked as well brushed as that of the Persian cat whose picture graces packets of toilet rolls. She was as haughty as a queen—and she was the most out-and-out coquette it has ever been my misfortune to meet.

—*What are you doing here?* she hissed malevolently.

—*Our human is coming to work with this crew*, I replied, not without the required deference; etiquette apart, it has always been my policy to pour oil on troubled waters.

—*Well, you needn't think you can get away with anything*, she snapped. —*You're not only the newest, but you're also way smaller than anyone else here, and you know where that puts you, don't you?*

I knew perfectly well what kind of "anything" I was not supposed to get away with. —*I have absolutely no intention*, I said with no little dignity, —*of being any other than my usual irreproachable self.* And I stuck my nose in the air and turned my face away to signify an unconcern that I was in fact far from feeling. But as I did so, I could not fail to catch her expression out of the corner of my eye. It was none other than pure and unsullied hate, although what competition she could ever have expected from such a model of decorum as me is hard to determine. But I suppose she was subject to the basic insecurity that anyone whose status is determined solely by their looks cannot help but feel.

When the pack had calmed down somewhat, Chris came back from the cookshack (with chocolate-chip-cookie breath) and unfastened Sport's chain. He at once hopped out and the clamour increased somewhat, but Sport was never an aggressive dog, and there was little altercation. Dreadlocks, despite his initial display of ferocity, had an uncanny ability to recognize when new members were accepted into the pack; once he had done so, he tolerated them completely, even when our combined human and canine numbers swelled to 50 or so, which they later did when we moved onto the mainland for the Interior planting season. Any stranger, however, was warned off in no uncertain terms; many Sunday drivers, arriving at our little lake to try their hand at fishing, took one look at the situation and gunned their motors to get out of there as fast as they possibly could.

When I thought no one was looking, I hopped down too, but I was not to get away completely unscathed and had to endure a few sharp nose jabs in a somewhat sensitive area before I was left alone. Queenie flirted disgracefully with a couple of the bachelors and pretended to ignore me, but I knew that much of her posturing was for my benefit alone.

Chris moved her truck back to the far end of the clearing, away from most of the other planters, as was her wont, and by the time she had pitched her heavy tree-planting tent and roofed it securely with a great blue tarp, the crummies were rolling into the yard and disgorging the planters. Tiredly they rescued their bags and shovels from the backs of their vehicles and straggled over to the shower tent to wash away the day's mud, duff and rain. They took little notice of us at first—they were tired and hungry, and new people at tree-planting camps are nothing unusual—but as they lined up for supper (baked salmon, focaccia and lasagne, no less!) and grouped themselves loosely about the tables or around the barrel stove, they started to ask Chris about herself.

I had come to realize by then that Chris's propensity for wilderness dwelling was considered quite abnormal among the rest of her species; moreover, it had occasioned her some notoriety. Chris revelled in this; despite her desire for solitude, once presented with an audience, willing or otherwise, she took great pleasure in showing off. She would pour out her life history with that peculiar brand of humility that people affect when they wish to appear modest but are in fact blatantly boasting of their accomplishments.

"You're an author, then?" said one of the planters politely. (*Cabin at Singing River*, Chris's first book, based on the letters she had written to the radio program, had been on the market for a year by that time.)

"You've built your own cabins all by yourself? A two-day hike from a road?" said another with a little more interest.

"I think I've heard of you," remarked a third. (At which Chris simpered dreadfully.) "Are you the one who writes letters to Peter Gzowski's *Morningside* on CBC Radio?"

"That's me," grinned Chris, glowing.

"Well, for gosh sakes," said the man. "We listen to Peter Gzowski all the time. Our whole community does. Most of us are craftsmen when we're not tree planting. We always have the CBC on while we work. And you're actually that person. That's amazing."

"I've heard you, too," said another planter delightedly. "I particularly liked that letter you sent about your dog running away when you were attacked by the bear."

"Thanks," Chris laughed. "That was Lonesome. She's sitting right there."

The first planter struck his forehead in absolute wonder. "I don't believe this," he exclaimed. "That's the dog? The very same dog that you wrote about? The dog that was on the radio?"

Chris nodded.

"That's astounding. I can't believe it!" he said again. "This is wonderful. I can't wait to go home and tell my wife that I've actually met a dog who was on Peter Gzowski!"

&

FOR PLANTERS WHO have cut their teeth in the interior of British Columbia, as Chris had, coast planting is a whole different ball game. Gone are the gentle slopes and burned, comparatively brush-less blocks, many of them ploughed with furrows, which enable the planter to slam in 2,000, 3,000 or even 4,000 seedlings a day. On the coast, the terrain is often as much vertical as horizontal—Chris crept around on cliffs that she would never have attempted to climb in the normal run of events, even though she was further hampered by bulging hip packs feathered with trees and a shovel she had to hang on to as well. The inevitable awkwardness of rain gear added to the difficulties, for it was usually precipitating in some form or another. If it wasn't raining, it was snowing, and the latter was always wet and soggy and made the ground very slippery. The stumps on the clear-cuts were monstrous, often two or three yards through. (What trees they must have been when they were alive!) Trees that were of species not deemed economical to market—such as yew, despite the wonderful drug extracted from that species as a cure for cancer—or that were the wrong dimensions for the very size-specific, automated mills, plus massive, twisted roots and severed limbs littered the site to such a degree that the planter sometimes walked high off the ground and had to drop periodically into holes to reach the earth. Chris was exhausted, aching and grumpy with the constant dreariness and wet, and I have no doubt she would have taken it out on Sport and me had we been within reach, but fortunately we were usually left in camp.

On the whole, Dreadlocks kept the camp fairly orderly. Apart from the heady charge at an intruder (in which I, needless to say, never participated) and a few minor squabbles over the leftovers, life progressed at an even and uncomplicated pace. The rain was tedious; I spent most of my time crawling under the truck for shelter, but when the rest of the pack were occupied in whatever crisis they deemed it necessary to police, I would sneak round to the back of the kitchen trailer where the cook, I knew, would give me an extra treat. Humans were always enamoured with my gentle and modest demeanour, and the cook and her helper were easily conned into thinking that because I was so much smaller than the rest of the pack, I was not getting enough to eat. (Chris, of course, kept dog kibble in the truck, but who on earth, if there was a choice, would want to eat that?)

Most humans treat dogs as toys; it never occurs to them that their canines might be happier with A Purpose in life. My prowess as a pack dog (even though I actually hated doing it) was received with some interest. Queenie's human in particular wanted to know what my saddlebags looked like, and when Chris produced them, he at once wished to try them on Queenie. This innocent incident was to have a very dramatic consequence.

Chris explained to the other planter that my backpack was too small for the malamute (and indeed the bags looked silly, like two pimples on a big, fluffy pumpkin) and demonstrated how the weight of the packs should sit firmly on the dog's shoulders and not in the middle of the back. Queenie laid back her ears a little, but otherwise, apart from a slight narrowing of her eyes, she stood quietly and made no fuss.

The instant that the backpack was removed, however, Queenie erupted into rage. And she directed this fury not at the humans who had subjected her to the indignity, but at me. With a maniacal howl she leapt upon me and proceeded to beat me up so severely that one of my ears was ripped to shreds and the blood poured down the side of my face.

I was shocked out of my wits. I had never, in my whole life, been attacked by another dog. It all happened so fast, I hardly had time to think. I certainly made no attempt to fight back. Humans were yelling; other dogs were barking and tearing along to join the fray; scenes of my childhood flashed before my eyes. It seemed an age, but in fact it couldn't have been more than a second or two before Queenie let go.

—*That'll teach you to try and dominate me, you miserable snivelling wimp*, she snarled.

—*It wasn't me,* I began, but when I saw another spark of anger flare in her eyes, I simply grovelled. Queenie's human had her on a lead by this time, and I made good my escape, spending the rest of the day hiding under a tool bench and wearing an expression that would be bound to elicit maximum human sympathy. Indeed, this was not difficult, for it was a major trauma to come to terms with such a violation of both my body and my mind. But it is the fashion these days to feel sympathy for the criminal rather than the victim; what is more, beauty creates its own standards of morality, and I spent the next several hours alone and in misery. So when, a couple of weeks later, a satellite crew of Chris, Sport, 10 other planters and

I were sent almost all the way across the top of Vancouver Island to the Atluck Valley, I was not too disappointed at leaving Woss and its attendant memories behind.

The Atluck was a heavily ravaged area that was notorious for its rock. Sometimes the most amazing razor-sharp pinnacles of limestone jutted forth from the monstrous tangle of slash (with microscopic patches of plantable soil at both the bottom and the top); at other times, huge, round sinkholes plunged deep into the earth like enormous vertical culverts. One had to be careful about jumping onto slash in that country; there might very well be nothing underneath.

This was a small camp by tree-planting standards. Being the only two dogs gave Sport and me an instant rise in status. We had a different cook, but she was no less an expert in the culinary art. She was, however, very strict about not allowing dogs into the cookshack. Chris herself had never encouraged this, and in most camps the rule was observed, but once the other planters found out how famous I was and how well-manneredly I conducted myself, many would sometimes sneak me into the cookshack when supper was over. I soon learned how to nudge open the screen doors with my nose and often spent the night beside the cooling stove. Chris was almost always the first planter up in the morning, and she would turf me out then. However, I quickly understood just how much leeway I was allowed, and when the new cook put her foot down, I obeyed her at once.

The Atluck camp had one major difference from all the others I ever lived in. We had a human baby for a pet. One of the planters had brought along his wife and infant child. Human children need a long period of development before they can walk, and this baby was still at the helpless stage. She sat and rocked in a little plastic bathtub that could either be perched on a table or strapped into the seat of a car. She was a cheerful infant, greeting all the planters with a great big grin and a chuckle every time they came through the door. Some of the other planters had children of their own, but even if their wives had wanted to come, only a babe in arms was safe in camp. Chemicals, unprotected stoves and sharp tools made too many hazards for toddlers. Thus many of the planters could see their families but rarely through the season, and competition to hold this baby was rife. But only among the men, oddly enough. Chris, the cook and the other two women planters never evinced any interest in cuddling the child. The young men, however—one of whom, although he had seen only 18 planting seasons himself, was the father of a two-year-old—sat around the stove at night and, instead of the usual planting, car, drug and vacation stories one heard in other camps, solemnly discussed teething, breastfeeding, diaper changing and sleepless nights.

I mention this child in some detail, for she had a bearing on an incident in which Sport was also a main participant.

The baby's mother helped the cook at times, but as it was a small camp, there was not a lot of work for her to do, and she used to go for long walks, carrying the baby in a little pack that hung in front of her chest.

One day Sport barked. I knew immediately, of course, what he was shouting about, and I at once checked around for a suitable refuge. But the cook was unfamiliar with Sport's habits (and Chris was on the block with the other planters so could not inform her), and she had no idea what had excited him. Because he otherwise barked so infrequently, she knew it must be something unusual.

"Perhaps it's an elk," she said. "One of those Roosevelt elk that are supposed to live around here."

"I'd love to see one," said the baby's mother, a city woman from Quebec. "I think I'll follow Sport and try and catch a glimpse of it." And with no further ado she strapped the baby onto her front and trotted off in the direction of the barking.

—*No! No! Don't go!* I tried to say. —*Sport wouldn't bark at an elk. There's only one thing he ever barks at like that!* But there was nothing I could do to stop her.

When Chris and the planters returned that evening, the child's mother was bubbling over with her adventures.

"I hit that patch of second growth over by that old pile of logging cables. It's so thick in there, it's like hair on a dog's back. I had to crawl on my hands and knees. And when I finally got to where Sport was barking, I saw he'd treed a bear! So there I was, on my hands and knees with the baby slung against my chest, a dangerous bear up the tree, and the only way out was to crawl backwards." And then she did a curious thing. Instead of reviling Sport for creating so much trouble, with a beatific smile on her face she cried out, "And Sport saved me! He kept on barking so the bear stayed up the tree while I was able to get away! What a good boy!"

I was dumbfounded. Saved you? I thought. He was the one who led you into danger in the first place! If he'd simply barked and stayed in camp as he should have done, none of this would have happened. The bear would have quietly gone away.

"And you should have seen Lonesome," said the young mother, turning to me and beginning to laugh. "You ought to have seen where she was! When we all came back, we found her curled into a tiny ball right under the furthest table of the cookshack! Thank goodness we have Sport to defend our camp! What a wonderful dog he is!" And she gave him an elaborate pat. And would you believe it, the rest of the humans (Chris excepted) followed suit.

I was pretty taken aback by this assessment of Sport's prowess. He was, after all, only being an idiot. A bark in camp to keep a bear away is one thing, but a deliberate antagonistic approach is plain foolhardiness. The child's mother had, I should add here, never seen a bear before in her life. And another thing: She herself was quick enough to run back to the shelter of the cookshack when she saw the bear. Why, therefore, shouldn't I?

Well, Sport enjoyed a bit of attention for a day or two, but I am afraid his elevated status was very short-lived. The next day the cook made a pot of spaghetti sauce that she intended to use later, and she put it outside to cool. Once again, Sport was the main performer in the drama that followed.

He ate the lot.

CHAPTER EIGHTEEN

THAT YEAR, ONE OF OUR planters got shot.

Coast planting ended around the middle of April, and after a much-needed week's rest, the crew reassembled in the extreme southeast corner of British Columbia to plant the mountainous finger of land known as the East Kootenays (actually part of the Rocky Mountains) that separates Alberta from the US border. The nearest town was Fernie; the camp was about 20 klicks east on an old landing reached by a logging road that ran through a brushy block. Casual traffic along the logging road was discouraged by a heavy bar fastened with a big padlock. Beside it was a large notice on which were the words NO SHOOTING. The area was a prime wintering ground for all manner of wildlife, and a major calving area for elk. Only those with special permission were supposed to be allowed to enter.

Chris had planned on being there early to help with the set-up of the camp, but the brakes on the truck failed (not for the first time, might I add: We once drove all the way down the switchbacks of The Hill without so much as a brake shoe or drum intact). Consequently, she spent most of the day and all her remaining cash at the gas station in Fernie. That truck was becoming a real liability. I tried to tell Chris that it was high time we got a new one, but as usual, she never took much notice of me. The radiator now leaked so badly it was irreparable, and my travelling water, as often as not, had to be used to keep it going. The truck consumed a quart of oil for every fill-up of gas; its exhaust system farted and popped with blatant indelicacy at the most inappropriate moments; it was almost impossible to start; and in instances like the brake failure, it was downright dangerous. On top of which, the rusted exterior and the tailgate, which was hung on with wire, were a distinct embarrassment in most circles—although they were not, I am afraid to say, particularly out of place in a tree-planting camp.

When we finally squeezed through the locked gate and trundled along the logging road, it hardly needed the bold arrow of flagging tape to show us that we had arrived, for long before we reached it, we passed the usual collection of trucks, tents, trailers and tarps. The cookshack had already been erected; it was a masterpiece of whimsy, for the landing had been ripped and seeded with grass after the loggers had finished with it, and the resulting tussocky surface was enormously uneven. The spine of the cookshack sagged like a sway-backed ewe, and the chimney shot askew out of the roof like a diver teetering on the edge of the board, past the point of no return. The floor of the shack, still smelling sweetly of crushed grass, sported a miscellany of folding tables propped at every angle and wedged precariously at their lower corners with lumps of wood. The cook and her helper were stripping the kitchen clean of the inch-thick layer of dust that had accumulated during the journey; a group of planters was trying to put together the jigsaw puzzle of the shower lean-to; and several others were digging holes for the outhouses, grey water and compost, or untangling plumbing hoses and lugging propane cylinders, the water filter, propane water heaters, the pump and the generator to their various stations. There was little left for Chris to do other than ease her vehicle onto a level patch of ground close to a creek, where it ran through a culvert (which, you may well imagine, I kept a very wary eye upon, especially when the peak of the spring flood occurred).

Most of the planting in the province took place during the month of May and the early part of June. Contracts at that time were close enough together that many could be completed from a single camp, and we were to be in this location for six weeks. The increased intensity of planting required a larger crew, and our human numbers swelled to more than 40 once university had finished; most crews, I was informed, were not as efficient as ours, needing 50 or 60 planters to do the same amount of work. Even 40 planters meant an uncomfortable crush on the facilities—but the leftovers were divine! Although there were now 10 other dogs to share them with, Sport and I feasted like kings.

It was an area that abounded with wildlife. Both mule deer and white-tailed deer proliferated, as well as moose and elk; once Chris, on her way home from a laundry day in town, screeched to a halt to excitedly observe two cougars who stared at us momentarily from the bush before vanishing. Some of the planters observed a pack of wolves loping through one of the blocks, and we had a resident porcupine right in camp. As you can imagine, I gave this creature a wide berth.

Bears, needless to say, were a fact of life.

Tree-planting camps are full of bear horror stories. With good reason, too, for planters have been mauled and even killed; some of our crew were actual witnesses to one of the latter tragedies. Fortunately, the only bear encounters we experienced were not too serious, but they were always cause for concern.

Fernie is a coal-mining district. Coincident with our arrival in the area, the mines went on strike. As this happened to be the spring bear-hunting season, thousands of impoverished miners roamed the country in their four-by-fours and ATVs, sporting their ostentatious weaponry and shooting at everything that moved.

Some of them were after victims other than bears. Not long after we arrived, one of the crews came upon a floppy-eared, liver-and-white hound padding exhaustedly along a logging road (on our side of the locked gate). Around the hound's neck was a bulky collar with a little stiff wire poking out of it.

"It's a radio collar," said one of the planters, surprised.

"That's the latest thing out here," explained another. "That's how they hunt cougar these days. They turn the dogs loose and track them; when the signal is stationary, they know the dog has treed a cougar, and they drive up and shoot it."

The dog was mournfully looking up at the truck. Someone opened the tailgate, and it hopped happily inside. The planters took it back with them to camp, and we dogs learned that he had been let out of his human's pickup that morning and had had a wonderful time running wherever he felt like it, but now he was very footsore and very hungry and a very, very long way from home. It was hard to feel too sorry for a dog who was allowed free rein of his baser instincts—and in a restricted wildlife area to boot—but he was a guest, and we canines had to stick up for our own. So we let him have a bowl of water and a little food.

An hour or two later a pickup arrived, and the driver, belly bulging like an inverted shelf over his pants' belt, laid claim to the dog. "I was only letting him run to give him some exercise," he muttered.

"Yeah, right!" said the planters, handing back the dog in disgust.

"We should have taken the collar off when we found the dog and just dropped it in the bush," said one of the planters after the man had gone.

"I would have tied it to a stick and thrown it into the river," said Chris darkly. "That would give them something to follow. It's pretty obvious which one of them needs the exercise."

But it was bears that the miners were really after. Apparently, their paws and gall bladders were fetching huge prices. Never a day went by without gunshots blasting off. We had barely set up camp before some out-of-work miners in a mega four-by-four with fat, thick-lugged mud tires rolled into camp.

"Hi," said the driver, without getting out of the vehicle.

Chris and one or two of the planters nodded a wary greeting.

"Seen any bears?" said the passenger.

"No!" said one of the planters emphatically. "And we wouldn't tell you if we did."

At which the visitors looked first amazed, then affronted and finally angry. Without another word, the driver gunned the motor, swung the wheel and roared off in a spurt of gravel.

We heard shots that evening and on and off during the following day. Four days later, two other miners came into camp. They gave the usual preliminary: "Seen any bears?" Then they added casually, "We wounded a grizzly just below your camp three days ago. It's pro'lly still aroun' here somewhere."

A grizzly? I thought, aghast. Wounded? Three days ago? And they never even told us? But that seemed to be the mentality of most of these so-called hunters.

A day or two later, the planters had another tale to tell. One of the crummies had come upon a truck with a big hunting mastiff tied in the back. The driver honked the horn, and everyone in the crummy yelled as loudly as they could to scare the bear away. After supper, this same truck rolled into camp, and a young man climbed out of the cab. (The dog, despite his size, was far too chicken to take on Dreadlocks and the rest of the pack, and he stayed in the back.)

"Thanks for screwing up my research," said the man, grinning. "I'm a bear biologist, and I was observing a sow with two cubs!" He asked the planters to take note of his truck and dog for the future.

But the bear hunters were at their most frightening when they staked out our camp.

When we first went to Fernie, it was still early enough in the year for it to be quite dark—and usually frosty—after supper. The planters would build a big fire in front of the cookshack and sit around banging, shaking and twanging a variety of noisemakers. Dogs would join the circle, me with my paws stretched out toward the fire.

It didn't take long for the bears to sniff out our temporary home. They were used to cleaning up garbage from the logging camps, so had learned that people mean food. When one came close, Dreadlocks and all the other canines would erupt into a cacophony of barking (I, of course, was far too ladylike to join in), and the whole pack would surge en masse into the darkness—where the bold, brave hunters were just waiting for something like this to happen. Headlights would flash on and guns would explode into the night. It was absolutely terrifying.

With so many guns popping off in all directions, and so many people occupying the region, it was perhaps not surprising that someone got in the way of a bullet.

The incident occurred during a day off. One of our planters, a young woman, had wandered down into a brushy block below camp to be alone for a while. It was a hot day and rather muggy, I remember, and the spindly aspens that clothed the clear-cut were just starting to leaf out. After a time the planter dozed, and then became disoriented when she wanted to return to camp. Hearing a car on the nearby road, she turned toward it; a shot rang out—and the next moment, she had a bullet in her foot.

She told us later that she was so shocked she didn't know what to do. But then she crawled to the road, where she was found by another planter who was just returning from town, so he was able to take her to the doctor.

The shooter was never found. The police took measurements; the distance the bullet had travelled, they said, was 400 yards. They figured, from the trajectory, that the most likely target had been the No Shooting notice, which must have been only three yards from the car.

And which, of course, the shooter had missed.

CHAPTER NINETEEN

BY THIS STAGE OF MY narrative, you are probably beginning to feel a little overwhelmed by the adventures I have related, and are perhaps even wondering if any dog could have had such a number of narrow escapes in a single life. But there is nothing in this account that is not the absolute truth; one should perhaps remember that these incidents did not happen all at once, but were spread out over a period of a dozen or more years.

In other words, by the time the planter was shot, I was no longer young. My hair had grown much longer and shaggier, and instead of being flecked with grey, as it was when I was a pup, it was now largely that colour alone, especially around my muzzle. I sported a handsome silver moustache that fluffed out over my lips, and great mop-like bangs that completely obscured my eyes if Chris neglected to cut them. (Ever since my brush with the baby porcupine, I have hated it when sharp tools come anywhere near me, but I have to admit, once the agonizing click is over, I do enjoy being able to see.) I was also getting a little stiff in the back legs; some of our longer expeditions would leave me sore for days. As Chris was similarly affected—did I tell you we reached middle age at approximately the same time?—she had perhaps less sympathy for me than she otherwise might have. At least she no longer made me carry heavy loads (although I was still entrusted with the most sensitive of her possessions: her flower-sketching equipment and even her camera at times), and in winter I never carried anything at all.

It was with some consternation, one February, that I observed Chris getting ready for a trip to the road. We didn't travel in and out on foot quite so often in winter by this time; we'd had a truly horrendous experience a couple of years previously when, instead of taking its usual three days, the journey became an ordeal that dragged on for six. The snow had been so deep and soft, and the wind so powerful, that on two of those terrible days we covered a grand total of five miles. On top of it all, Chris had not budgeted for a six-day journey, and we had carried only three days' food, so rationing, for all of us, was a trial in itself. There were times on that trip when I was simply ready to curl up into a ball in the snow and stay there. It was only my innate obedience that kept me struggling after Chris at all. When she had seen the difficulty I was having, she had hoisted my pack on top of hers, but I really did not think at the time that we would ever come out of the mountains alive. Admittedly, that fiasco had been much earlier in the winter, when travel conditions were more uncertain, and Chris, by her own later admission, had made a very bad decision as to the route. But she was always taking "shortcuts" that landed us into terrible trouble, and our six-day marathon was an experience I had no wish to repeat.

So when the root cellar was checked for mouse holes, and all the remaining vegetables, cans and jars were incarcerated in it; when the chimneys were swept, the shutters put up, the fuel stored out of reach of bears, and the backpacks and toboggans patched and renovated and loaded with supplies, I awaited my fate with great trepidation.

At least, I thought with relief as we set off, we were not going to attempt the high route along which we had gotten into so much trouble before. This time, the only climbing we did was up the small rise behind the extreme eastern corner of the lake, after which we dropped quickly down the narrow little gully that led to Avalanche Lake.

The original trap trail that we were following had been blazed a generation before and had not been maintained since. Now brush and windfall blocked it, and in some instances the marked trees themselves had fallen over. Chris and I had travelled this route numerous times, in both summer and winter, but Chris had still never managed to stay on the trail the whole way. (If she'd had a better nose, she'd have had no problem.) But of course she never took my advice, and we inevitably ended up doing a lot of frustrating floundering and bush-bashing before we reached the logging road.

Nothing untoward happened until we arrived at the foot of Avalanche Lake, several hours along our route. Beaver had dammed the creek near its exit from the lake, and this is where Sport ran into trouble.

Ice on beaver ponds is always suspect, for the constant movement of the animals beneath it keeps the surface thin. Despite the recent cold spell, this pool was already partly open, and I knew well enough to follow Chris in the deep snow on the bank and leave the ice alone.

Not so Sport, however. He ran out onto it. Chris called him back, and he obeyed promptly, but just as he was about to step onto the shore, in he went. Because of his heavy pack (he was carrying an enormous load; Chris had allowed me to make this trip unladen, and Sport received the brunt of the extra weight), he was unable to pull himself out. Needless to say, his vociferation at this predicament was delivered at an impressive level of decibels.

Chris tramped to the edge of the bank as swiftly as she could, but the depth of snow and resistance of the snowshoes prevented her from reaching Sport. So she kicked the snowshoes off with the idea that she would sink farther into the snow and thus be able to get her fingers around Sport's collar. The plan worked well enough—she sank beautifully. Unfortunately, there was no land under the snow at that point, and she too ended up in the water.

She half fell against the bank, and this supported her body, but Sport at once thrust his weight against her and prevented her from moving. She sat there, cursing and swearing, water pouring into her boots, while she undid Sport's belly strap and yanked his pack over his head. The yelling stopped abruptly, and Sport frantically clawed his way onto dry land. As his front paws were already in Chris's lap, his most direct route to safety was right over her body. I could hear his heavy wet paws scrabbling against the fabric of her coat. Then, before Chris could move or expostulate, Sport did what all dogs do when first coming out of the water: He shook himself. As he was standing about six inches from Chris's left ear at the time, I will let your own imagination fill in the resulting comments that blistered through that quiet and snowy world.

Well, it was not the first time Chris had gone through the ice, and she had spare felt liners and socks in her pack, so there was no great harm done. I was pleased to see that she made Sport carry the wet ones. Neither was it very cold, for by now the temperature had warmed to just below freezing. Indeed, although it was still shady along the river, fingers of sunlight were turning the treetops to gold. As we entered the next stretch of forest, we experienced a very unwelcome side effect to the sun's largesse.

During the cold spell of the previous few days, it had snowed a lot. At this elevation (quite a bit lower than that of our cabin), it had been comparatively windless. Great fluffy piles, therefore, sat on all the trees. All of a sudden, they began to loosen and cascade off the branches in monstrous, powdery, white waterfalls. Every few yards we were simply deluged in snow. Chris yelled as fearsomely as Sport when the huge snow bombs pummelled her back and poured down her neck. Grumblingly she pulled her rain jacket (for it had become too warm to walk in a coat) over her head and shoulders to protect her from the onslaught. Because I was too well mannered to voice my discomfort, she never gave a thought to me until, at one point, she happened to turn around and see me plodding faithfully at her heels. In her usual heartless fashion, she burst into peals of laughter. I was so drowned in snow that my shaggy mop of fur had turned completely white.

We came to another lake. Below the outlet of this one there was a river crossing. Sometimes we had had to wade through the water here even in the winter, but thanks to the previous cold weather, the crossing was nicely frozen. Shortly afterward, the sun dipped behind the mountain and it was time to make camp. Chris chose a big spruce for the dense shelter it gave, but she had not bargained for the quantities of snow still sitting in the branches. As the warm air from the fire hit the snow, it turned to water and dripped. The sky was absolutely clear and full of stars, but we sat with a tarp over our heads in our own column of rain.

Close to the end of the afternoon on the following day, we reached Charlotte Lake. We passed Ookpik's deserted cabin—there was never anyone there in winter—and soon encountered snow-machine trails that took us easily to the nearest logging road. And so, despite the snow-bomb passage, the journey had not been all that bad. I had no way of knowing that it was to be the last winter trip I would ever make.

*The collection of humans and animals at Schoolhouse
Creek made for a large and boisterous mélange.*

CHAPTER TWENTY

AT THIS POINT IN THE story, I must backtrack a bit again and tell you about Schoolhouse Creek.

I think I have mentioned that Chris fancied herself an artist. Periodically, she would have shows, at which she hoped to make a bit of extra income by selling pictures that she had painted. At one of these shows, when I was still quite young, she met a man called Hans. He invited her home to meet his pack—and that was how Schoolhouse Creek entered our lives.

It was about six hours' drive from Nimpo Lake, and my first impression of the place, after we had bowled along the inevitable dusty logging road that serviced it (almost all of Chris's friends seemed to live in these out-of-the-way places), was that it housed the biggest bunch of geriatrics I had ever seen in my life. There were two old dogs (one of them positively doddery); an octogenarian horse; a bunch of sheep trailed after by an impotent ram; a male goose, nominally in charge of two females, but well into his dotage; two senile cats; and several chickens running loose with a decrepit rooster—it was a constant puzzle to me why they had not been consigned to the pot long ago. The pack also included an old human gentleman who walked stiffly on crutches and was to eventually live beyond his 90th birthday. Other animals included a flock of ducks; meat rabbits in a cage; a huge, goofy younger mutt called Oscar, who possessed not a vestige of manners but was foolish enough to be winkled out of his basket quite easily; three younger horses; a multitude of half-tame wild birds who were constantly provided with fat in winter and seeds in summer; and a large number of human and dog visitors and other hangers-on. Needless to say, it all amounted to a large and boisterous mélange, a different environment to the one Chris affected at home.

The alpha female presiding over this entourage was a human who, like me, must have been the runt of her litter, but who possessed the biggest heart it has yet been my lot to experience. She was an absolute darling; all the animals, and the people, loved her unreservedly. She was also the best cook in the world—tree-planting caterers not excepted (or was it just that my own human's culinary efforts left so much to be desired?). You should have seen the treats we dogs got! Cream, yogurt and cottage cheese made all the more delectable by long periods of storage in the fridge. Bones and meat scraps galore, for the humans butchered the sheep and chickens themselves. Leftover stews; salmon pies and pizzas made with homemade dough. Even the bread crusts were so full of grains that they were meals in themselves. There were also numerous vegetable dishes and salads constructed from produce grown in the large garden that sprawled beneath the road, if you happened to like that sort of thing. I was more than happy to allow the rabbits and chickens their share of this part of the meals.

Tina (which was the alpha female's name) was always totally unbiased toward any of her pack and treated us all with an equality that was embarrassing at times, for one of the hard facts of life is that every animal should learn to know its place. I was never quite able to reconcile myself to being considered at the same social level as the chickens.

The setting of the little farm was delightful. The collection of sun-reddened log buildings and sagging split-rail fences trickled down a sunny slope (in a much kinder climate than that of Chris's chosen domiciles) and looked over a wide valley containing a mixture of fields, swamp and deciduous as well as coniferous forest, with distant vistas of mountains as a pretty background setting (which is where mountains should be).

Dominating the life of both the valley and the farm was the river. It was as wide and swift as the one that ran in front of our cabin near Lonesome Lake. The river into which Schoolhouse Creek ran was, however, much farther away from the sea; despite this, it was also a salmon-spawning stream. The fall was redolent with decaying fish, and before the spring flood, the exposed sweeps of sand and gravel turned into delectable snack bars full of scraps of crunchy bone and skin. Oddly enough, although the animals and their paw prints were seen on the gravel bars, bears were never a problem here.

Often, we would jump in the canoe and float down the river. Sport had to be left at home on these occasions as he was simply a nuisance with his howling; I was allowed my customary place in the boat, and Oscar swam noisily behind or galumphed in great bounds alongside, his long, wet, black hair spraying sheets of water as he ran. On other occasions, we dogs would all accompany the humans when they rode on horseback—what lovely excursions they were, up through the mixed aspen and spruce forest behind the house.

Tina, like Chris, was an artist. But instead of making various marks and incomprehensible scribbles on paper, she preferred to work with a rather peculiar kind of earth that came wrapped in plastic and packaged in cardboard boxes. She shaped and cajoled it into a number of shapes, usually portraits of animals. Some of these were exotic and I did not recognize them, but others were based on the animals that either surrounded or resided on the farm; many a sheep and chicken did duty as a model before it was eaten. Once the sculptures were shaped, she let them dry, then did extraordinary things with them using bitter-smelling chemicals, incredibly fierce ovens, fire and smoke. It all had the astonishing aura of necromancy; the results bore colours such as were never seen in real life, but the public must have loved them, for everything she made was exchanged for money, and she continuously made more and more and invented bigger and bigger designs. She ended up employing an army of assistants to keep the operation going.

To my unutterable delight, Chris began to spend more and more time at Schoolhouse Creek, usually in the fall, and sometimes in the spring on the way to and from tree-planting camp. As you can imagine, a place like that required much hard work to keep it going. While she stayed there, Chris resurrected her farming skills and spent a lot of time mending fences, shearing sheep, digging the huge vegetable gardens in the spring, shovelling manure and doing the daily rounds of feeding all the creatures, which was quite a performance, as every species seemed to need a different kind of food. But I think the real reason she stayed was because, like everyone else, she enjoyed being pampered. Chris was not getting any younger either, and she was finally beginning to see, very belatedly, the wisdom of a bit of luxury once in a while. She helped Tina with her artwork on occasion and, once she had the feel of the clay, was soon making sculptures of her own. Once, she fashioned a model of me. It was only a small sculpture, one that she could easily enclose within her hands, but although I say it myself, it was quite a good effort, and she managed to catch the nobleness of my expression fairly well.

Ah, Utopia! But nothing, alas, is perfect, and even this paradisical Eden was flawed. One of the disadvantages was the road. It ran directly below the buildings, separating the living area from the rest of the farm. It was used principally by logging trucks, which thundered by long before the first light squeezed into the sky and kept roaring past until well after dark. At the peak of the season they would barrel along at 20-minute intervals, day and night; Chris was nearly driven mad by them, although Tina and her mate had become somewhat used to them and had learned to accept them as part of their existence.

At first I was delighted with the road. In my younger days, you will remember, I always lived or stayed some distance from a highway. Even Tan Sister's home at Stuie was separated from the road by a long and bumpy driveway. Consequently, I had come to associate the sound of an approaching vehicle with a visitor, the greeting of whom was always—and still is—my favourite occupation. Thus, when I first arrived at Schoolhouse Creek, every time I heard a motor I would run onto the road to greet it. But these vehicles never stopped. At best, my advances were reciprocated by ear-shattering engine-reduction eructations, spitting gravel and clouds of choking dust; at worst, they inspired squeals of tire rubber and an irate stream of human invective as the truck thundered by. If Chris saw me heading for the gateway, she would screech at me like a nutcracker; even Tina, who did not have it in her to harden her voice, spoke to me quite firmly on these occasions. So gradually I learned that vehicles and visitors were not always compatible and that the former had to be avoided; indeed, it sometimes took a not-inconsiderable amount of acumen to cross the road to the garden and still retain a modicum of dignity.

The other great disadvantage of Schoolhouse Creek was its wildlife. Not the inconsequential little birds that busied themselves around the feeder or surreptitiously swiped grain from in front of the stupid hens' noses, but the large animals that abounded in the area, for, like Lonesome Lake, Schoolhouse Creek was a haven for predators. Coyotes were common, and a large number of the domestic ducks, geese, sheep and chickens fell prey to these hooligan gangs. Occasionally, touring mobs of wolves would join in the slaughter, although they generally confined their activities to wilder prey. Once, a group of ducks housed in an empty hen barn for the winter were demolished by a skunk—Hans shot the perpetrator, but the stink hung about the building for years, and when Chris shovelled the manure out of it, as she did every spring, the reek of the skunk clung to her clothes for weeks.

Tina made part of her living by selling her artwork at craft fairs; Chris, figuring that this might be yet another way to make a much-needed dollar, tried her hand at printmaking (a different way of making marks on paper) and took her work to the fairs as well. She was never very successful financially (although when her books started to be published, she did a lot better), but as it was extremely difficult to get in and out of Nuk Tessli at that time, we stayed at Schoolhouse Creek between fairs.

In later years, we hung on until Christmas. (Turkey skin! Ham bones! Stuffing and roast potatoes! Fridge-fermented gravy!) Although Schoolhouse Creek had a much kinder climate than Nuk Tessli, there was usually snow on the ground at that time, and it was on one of those occasions that a serious incident occurred, which nearly cost both Sport and Oscar their lives.

Once they got to know each other, Oscar and Sport became quite good buddies (their mental capacities were somewhat on a par). It was never clear who the instigator was, for neither would roam far on his own, but I am afraid to say that together they took to cruising the countryside, and they would sometimes be gone for hours. One day, the local outfitter came by and said he'd seen their tracks in the snow—they had been chasing deer. He gave Chris and Tina warnings and said that if they did not control their dogs, he would be obliged to shoot them.

Well, this was Oscar's place, and as he was fine on his own, it was Sport who had to be confined. At that time, the oldest resident dog had gone to the great dog pound in the sky. In his day he had also been an incorrigible hunter, and the woodshed had been walled with chain-link fence so that he would have a bit of area to move in as well as a good shelter for his kennel. Sport was promptly confined here at night. And you can imagine how he voiced his protest at this restriction. In an effort to shut him up, to my everlasting and undying shame, I was thrust into the cage as well.

Now, I had never credited Sport with much ingenuity, but the lengths to which he would go to escape this confinement were unbelievable. He learned to climb up precarious piles of firewood and squeeze through the gap at the top of the wire, which one would not have thought able to accommodate a mouse. When these holes were blocked, he would work away at the boarded end of the woodshed until he had loosened a plank sufficiently to get through. As often as not, his escape would take him no farther than the porch of the cabin in which Chris slept. But when the moon was right and the deer were running, off he and Oscar would go.

Then one afternoon, the pair of them came home with blood on their muzzles and down the front of their chests. Tina was appalled, and she clutched at Oscar's collar. "What have you done?" she wailed. "What have you done?" Then, shocked, she turned to her husband. "It's sheep. He smells of sheep." Aghast, we all crossed the road in the direction from which they had come, picked up the tracks in the snow and followed them a short distance below the road, where there lay a bloody woollen carcass. Everyone stared down at it in frozen horror. Dogs who became livestock killers were sentenced to instant death.

"It's been dead a day or two by the smell," said Chris cautiously. "And look. Those tracks are old and snowed-on, but there seems to have been something staggering down from the road with an uneven gait. I bet the sheep got through the fence and was hit by a truck. It made it down here before it died, and the dogs must have found it already dead."

Well, this was serious enough, but not as bad as having murderers to contend with. Oscar and Sport confirmed to me that the animal had indeed expired long before they had found it; fortunately, the humans also accepted the scenario, and everyone breathed a sigh of relief.

Things went well for a few days, and people began to relax. Then another sheep was found dead, this time hard against the fence of the night paddock. Nearby were tracks in the snow that were almost as large as a wolf's, but a little more elongated, like a dog's. A strange aroma, with which I was only vaguely familiar, hung about the carcass.

"It's got to be Oscar and Sport!" thundered Hans. (The sheep were his particular project, and he was very proud of his small flock.)

"But Sport was shut in the woodshed all night," Chris protested. "I know he's been getting out and might have easily done it again, but he was inside the woodshed this morning, and he would certainly not have gone back there on his own."

"And Oscar hasn't been out of my sight for a minute," Tina stated firmly. "When he hasn't been kept in the porch of the house, he's been in my studio." But Hans was not convinced.

"It has to be the dogs. Look at the tracks. They're far too long for a wolf's and way too big for a coyote. I'll give you one more chance. If you cannot control the animals better, they are going to have to be shot." And with that, he stormed off in dreadful dudgeon.

"I know that Oscar was with me every minute during the last 24 hours," said Tina worriedly.

"I can account for Sport as well," said Chris. "But Hans is right. The tracks aren't from any of the wild dogs. Perhaps the neighbours' dogs have taken to roaming and killing animals. Packs of domestic dogs are far more likely to do that than wild animals anyway."

The next day, another sheep lay belly up against the fence; courtesy of a fresh fall of snow, it was possible to see that the whole flock had galloped madly in circles in their panic. Once again the dog-like prints were noticeable, but outside the paddock fence the horses had churned the snow, and the perpetrator could not be followed.

Sport and Oscar protested their innocence, but Hans was furious, and it was in fear and trembling that I awaited his judgment. Fortunately, he was persuaded that our dogs had been thoroughly controlled. "Then it's got to be a neighbour's dog," he growled. "We'll shut the sheep up in the barn tonight. I hate to do it if they're not lambing—there's not enough room for them all in there."

There will be soon, I thought privately, if this slaughter continues.

So that evening, all us dogs were shut up into porches and kennels, and the humans went down to drive the sheep into the barn. It took them a very long time, and a great deal of shouting and swearing could be heard through the wintry dusk. But eventually the humans came back, bad tempered and grumpy. "It's going to be a goddamn nuisance if we have to do this every night," Hans muttered darkly.

Would you believe that another sheep was killed that night? We were all dumbfounded. The killer had leapt right over the lower half of the barn door and dragged the sheep out with it.

"Surely no dog could ever do that!" Hans exclaimed in astonishment.

Chris and Tina stared at him with open mouths.

"It's like a spirit," said Tina with wonder.

"The Hound of the Baskervilles!" stated Chris tightly. (I think I have told you of her predilection for detective fiction.)

"That settles it," said Hans angrily. "I'm going to spend the night in the barn with the gun. We'll get that bastard yet."

And come nightfall, that was what he did. He dressed himself warmly, took a blanket, a thermos of tea and a camp chair, and sat with the sheep in the barn. During the night I awoke to the shrill ululation of coyotes. The moon was not far from full, and its brilliance poured like quicksilver over the snowy forests and fields. The river exhaled ghostly mists into the pale, frosty darkness. I imagined Hans sitting resolutely in the barn, the steamy press of woolly sheep murmurous about him, rifle at the ready, facing the upper half of the barn door that was open to the moon.

But of course nothing happened. Hans came grouchily in to breakfast, dopey with lack of sleep and shivering with cold.

"There's fresh tracks beside the most recent carcass," he said as he wolfed his tea and oatmeal. "They must have been made just before dawn; there was a small snowfall then. I'm going to follow them and see what I can find."

And he was gone for no more than a couple of hours before the boom of the rifle floated down the valley toward the house.

When he returned, he was grinning. The aroma I had been aware of around the carcasses was strong upon his clothes, noticeable even above the hated smell of cordite. "I got it," he said proudly. "Guess what it was."

Tina and Chris looked mystified.

"A cougar," Hans stated triumphantly. I blanched. A couple of humans had recently been killed by cougars, so their exploits had made the human news broadcasts.

"I've only caught glimpses of them before," said Chris. "We don't have them at Nuk Tessli. I'd love to have a look at it." And we all trooped along the river to see.

There were the great round front paws and the curiously elongated back ones that had left prints so like a dog's. And there was the great tawny cat face, eyes glazed, lips slightly open, teeth bared in an unconscious grimace of death. The long, lean body lay on its side, and the whip-like tail looped on the snow behind it. There was very little blood; the bullet had entered the heart.

I stared at it long and hard, committing the unfamiliar shapes and smells to memory. Even though it was dead, I still felt a frisson of fear—and with due reason, it turned out, for there was a consequence to this event that was to cause me hardship for the rest of my life.

I was concentrating so hard on examining the creature that I was only half-listening to what the humans were saying. Hans, apparently, was demonstrating how he stalked and shot the animal. He must have got carried away with his telling, for without any prior warning whatsoever, he lifted the gun to his shoulder and fired.

It was one of the most stunning things that has ever happened to me. Pinwheels of light flashed on and off in my head, and the noise was like a lance in my ears. Without stopping to think, I bolted for home.

All day I lay in a hole under one of the cabins. I was at first surprised, and then considerably hurt, that no one came by to look for me. Everyone seemed to have deserted the place; there were no chickadees, cats, dogs, humans or chickens. I lay in my little lonely ball and whimpered to myself, the sound ringing strangely in my head.

As it grew dark, I became hungry despite myself. Cautiously I felt my way out of the hole and across the yard. A great silence had descended on the place, as if it had been smothered in a thick blanket of snow. But no fresh snow had fallen since that morning, and the almost-full moon was already showing above the river in a sky that was frosty and clear.

And there was Chris, looking concerned and holding my dog dish. She moved her lips and seemed to say, "There you are, Lonesome. Where on earth have you been? I was worried about you." But no sound issued from her mouth.

The boom of the rifle had turned me completely deaf.

CHAPTER TWENTY-ONE

FORTUNATELY, THE TOTAL DEAFNESS LASTED only a few days, but there was always an underlying buzzing in my head, and my hearing never fully recovered. I determined this by Chris's expression when she was calling me from a distance. The instant I heard my name, I would run to her happily as usual, but her face would be red with anger and effort, the way it was when she was screaming at Sport to SHUT UP. I came to realize that she must have been calling for some time, but I soon learned that my habitual expression of innocence and slight puzzlement at her anger quickly disarmed her, indeed caused her to look somewhat contrite. I must confess that just once in a while I used this to my advantage. If I was involved in something particularly interesting, I could afford to allow a couple of yells to go by unacknowledged, and I knew that Chris would put it down to my imperfect hearing. But I did not use this device too often, as I felt guilty about it. I have always taken pride in my truthfulness and obedience (as I think I have mentioned before), and despite being sorely tried at times, I don't think I have disgraced myself at all in this respect—at least when I could avoid it. But aren't all of us allowed to bend the rules a little as we grow older?

In no time at all, tree-planting season was upon us again. How time seemed to fly! That spring we were placed with a different crew; once again we worked around the reservoirs north of Revelstoke, although many miles away from where I had had the brush with the porcupine.

What a ravaged landscape that was. Logged by the small-business program, which is the most destructive kind of forest tenure, it was a classic pattern of ill-planned roadbuilding (the steep, machine-churned hillsides were simply sliding into the reservoir), waste and lack of forethought. There wasn't an old-growth tree in sight.

I heard Chris say many times that it was to be her last year; she was never going to go tree planting again. She had said that during the blacker moments of almost every one of the seven years we had done this work, but this time there was a certainty about it that had not been there before. And when we finally drove away from camp early one clear summer morning, I knew by the lift in her face that this part of her life was behind her.

She had only stuck it out the final year because (as she frequently said) she really needed the money. (But when did she not?) However, this year I saw a concrete reason for her efforts to acquire some cash; she finally broke down, got rid of the old, ailing monster truck and bought a new one.

Not brand new, of course. It was sitting in a used-car lot in Revelstoke. A little tawny thing that handled like a car and purred sweetly like a contented cat. In fact, the motor was so quiet compared with the great red behemoth, which was the only one of Chris's vehicles I had known, that when it was idling at a traffic light I could no longer hear it and was often fooled into thinking that it was turned off and we had arrived at our destination.

The old wreck was sold to one of the planters for $500. He was a kindly young man with a long mane of black hair and features that might have been part Japanese and part native Indian. Chris told him all the things that she knew were wrong with the truck: poor starter, no muffler, wrecked radiator and several other things that I have since forgotten. But the brakes and tires had recently been fixed, the steering was fine, and the motor ran well. The young man liked the old red monster because, he said, in five years' time it would be 20 years old and therefore classed as an antique. He liked doing up old trucks. Lovingly, he wet his finger and wrote "Please" and "Me" in the dust on the tailgate on either side of the manufacturer's name. (It was a Dodge.)

Some months later, Chris, by chance, met another planter from that crew. "You know that old truck of yours?" he guffawed. "It's somewhere in the Fraser Canyon, so I hear. The motor blew on it. Poor Gerry never even got it home!"

Chris was both relieved and appalled—relieved that she had unloaded the vehicle so propitiously, and appalled that the young man had ended up with such a lemon. Perhaps that was the real reason why she never went tree planting again.

🍂

AND SO BACK to Nuk Tessli to prepare for another round of bugs, wildflowers, backpacking and our usual scattering of tourists. One morning, I trotted down to the lake to get a drink and slipped on a rock. In an effort to save myself from falling into the water, I must have done something to my back. I fell in anyway—trust the water monster to have the last word—and I seriously wondered if I was ever going to pull myself out again. I finally managed to drag myself onto the shore, but I could barely walk.

Chris was all concern; she felt my body thoroughly but could find no swelling or breaks and didn't know what to do to make me better. We certainly could not walk out to the vet, and the new vehicle had left her so broke that she had no money to hire a plane. Fortunately, we had no major hiking plans for the next few days, and by the time the first tourists of the season came, I was able to get about quite well. However, Chris divided the load that I would normally have carried between Sport and herself, and she never put a pack on me again. Thus, during that summer, the long hikes we took above the treeline were for me among the most carefree since my puppy days.

That fall we repaired, as usual, to Schoolhouse Creek to participate in the craft-fair circuit. Tina, Jasmine (who was her assistant at the time) and Chris would load their vehicles with all manner of diverse paraphernalia (apart from innumerable boxes, there was a multitude of puzzling bits of wood constantly referred to as "the booth") and take off for several days, leaving us dogs and the rest of the menagerie in the sole care of Hans.

Now here is a story that Tina loves to tell. Whenever she went away, she cooked a complete menu for her husband and his elderly father and left it all in the fridge or the freezer. The containers were labelled "Saturday supper," "Sunday lunch" and the like. One day, visitors arrived and Hans grabbed a big pot of stew, fragrant with meat and thickened with oats. He warmed it up and served it to his guests. "This is not of Tina's usual standard," he apologized to his visitors. "I can't understand why she would leave us this stuff." Nonetheless, they ate it all with gusto, some of the guests coming back for three helpings. When Tina came home, she found that a large casserole labelled "Friday dinner" was untouched. "What's the point of me cooking all these meals for you if you don't eat them?" she complained.

"But we ate what you left us," Hans insisted.

"At least," said Tina, surveying the large cleaned pot beside the sink, "you remembered to give the oats and butchering scraps to the dogs."

Chris and Tina were away most weekends during November and

early December of that year. Then Chris packed up the truck and we drove back to Nimpo for two weeks, returning to Schoolhouse Creek for Christmas. There were other people there and other dogs too, so it was quite a party all round. Fresh snow fell on Christmas morning, and the world was dazzling in the low winter sun. We had a wonderful walk along the sparkling, frozen river, just long enough to work up a perfect appetite for dinner.

After Christmas, Chris spent a day at the stores in Williams Lake, coming back in her usual foul mood, for she hated shopping with a passion. Imagine my surprise upon going up to the vehicle to greet her (fair mood or foul, I would never have neglected my duty) and smelling another dog inside the cab.

And to my horror, out jumped a bear! But no, she was not a bear; she just looked like one. She was enormous—quite a bit bigger than Sport, and just as tall and much rounder than Oscar. She had a great black, fluffy coat and round, stick-up ears. She had come, I was able to ascertain during the short time I conversed with her, from a large pack of sled dogs. She had lamentably few manners— when Chris offered her a smidgeon of turkey skin, she nearly took Chris's fingers off when she snapped at it. But that, I suppose, is what comes of having to fight for your food among a whole mess of belligerent canines.

I still had no intimation of what was in store for me. But the next morning, when Chris made the usual farewell noises to our hosts, it was The Bear who was coaxed into the back of the truck with Sport. I thought at first that I was to be awarded the privilege of riding in the cab, but instead Chris turned to me and said, "Stay, Lonesome. You've got to stay."

To say that I was puzzled would be an understatement. The hated word "stay" was bad enough in itself. But this time it had

*One day Chris brought home The Bear—a great
black sled dog with lamentably few manners.*

been spoken in a tone I had never heard Chris use before, a mixture of the fondness she so rarely expressed, tinged with a sorrow I could not define. She reached out her hands and tousled my bangs. "Stay," she said very softly. "Stay."

Abruptly, she turned and swung herself into the seat. "I'm out of here!" she called fiercely to her hosts. The motor fired, hand farewells were exchanged, and the truck, containing Chris, Sport, the winter's food supplies and The Bear, bumped slowly down the driveway and onto the road. Now, Chris had often left me at Schoolhouse Creek before, but never when she had taken Sport with her. And as I stood in the yard looking after her, sadly wagging my tail at half-mast, I knew in my heart that this was to be a very different kind of goodbye.

CHAPTER TWENTY-TWO

ONE CAN LOOK AT RETIREMENT in two ways: either regretfully, bewailing one's lost past, or as a new phase of one's life, looking forward to the discoveries and pleasures that a far less strenuous existence entails. I suppose most of us, no matter how positive we seem to be, steer a path somewhere between the two, the swing of the pendulum depending largely upon one's health.

There is no doubt that as a retirement home, Schoolhouse Creek cannot be beat. Tina loves all her charges unreservedly, and there is not a single animal in the place who does not reciprocate with equal fervour, no matter what our differences might be—and let me tell you, there are some pretty strong-willed and eccentric individuals in this place. But we all strive to get on with each other because of Tina's unswerving affection. She is the kind of person in whom it is impossible to imagine any vindictiveness; she is fair-minded with her largesse, and treats are spread equally all round (although once in a while I have noticed that Oscar gets an extra tidbit or two, great galumphing half-wit that he is). After a long life of deprivation and loneliness, I am surrounded by company and fed to my heart's content. We frequently set off on wonderful expeditions that are neither dangerous nor too strenuous, either through the forest behind the house or over the fields alongside the river, where humans, dogs and horses participate with equal enjoyment. (Although horses must be among the most pea-brained individuals on this earth; they desire nothing more than to do something new and exciting, but the moment they are out, the only time they show pleasure is when they are galloping headlong in the direction of home. But I forget myself . . .)

So life at Schoolhouse Creek is really ideal. Oscar is easily manipulated out of his basket; I can always intimate that something exciting is about to happen, upon which he leaps out of bed, leaving it not only vacant, but also pre-warmed. And you can imagine that I am not so easily duped; once I am in it, little can make me budge. Then there are the treats like gravy and commercially canned offal that is mixed with our kibble every night. Considerable dexterity is required on Tina's part to ensure that each animal gets its own dish and doesn't fight, especially when other dogs are visiting, which happens quite often. There are rarely fewer than three or four vehicles in the yard and half a dozen humans sitting round the table at Schoolhouse Creek. (Needless to say, this makes for a quantity of leftovers and scraps. Would that Chris had been more genial and had more visitors or a family of her own. Until I began to associate with other humans, I had no idea how Spartan our diet had been.)

So one would think that a dog in such circumstances could be nothing but content. And yet such is the capriciousness of the reasoning mind that there are times when I think of my old life with a kind of wistfulness I would not have believed myself capable of. I miss Chris, of course, although she has done little to deserve such longing. But despite her perverse idiosyncrasies, she has been the mainspring of my life ever since I was taken from my mother. One gets used to a relationship, no matter how abusive, and although Tina lavishes endearments upon me in a manner that Chris was never able to do, Chris had a certain directness about her—might I say doggedness?—that proffered its own kind of comfort. She was a strict taskmistress, but at least I always knew exactly where I stood with her. Beneath all her selfish desires and aspirations there was an underlying solidity and loyalty that I cannot deny. I even find that I miss Sport a little (although I have no such inclinations toward The Bear—the bitch!), and to my enormous surprise I miss Nuk Tessli and the great unfriendly acreage that surrounds it. When the logging trucks groan and roar, and the pickups full of snowmobiles thunder up the valley to mar the fresh, snowy winter mornings, fleeting visions flit through my head. Of the clear songs of fox sparrows bouncing back and forth over the mirror-calm morning lake while tendrils of mist writhe palely, like attenuated hands reaching to a cloudless sky; of the wide, high meadows rioting with flowers and fed by the melting snows; and of the spiralling eagles riding the thermals far beneath our feet as we stand upon a clean-swept summit and feel as though we are part of the wind.

Not long after I first visited Schoolhouse Creek, the oldest dog, Fritz, grew feeble. We had been out for a winter walk, and he simply lay down in a nest in the snow and would not move. He was still alive, but instead of bringing him home, Hans came back to the house and hung the rifle over his shoulder (upon which I retired at once into my safe hole beneath the studio). There was a distant shot, and then silence. We never saw Fritz again. Then Banner, the other old dog, grew very ill. Once again Hans took the rifle and came back smelling of cordite and newly turned earth. The geriatric horse died, and one day the old gentleman human also disappeared—I heard he spent a long time at the vet's; he never came home again either. Schoolhouse Creek was growing emptier, for none of these animals were replaced.

But otherwise, life flows easily. Chris still comes for long visits, and she brings Sport with her as well. Then it is almost like old times, for the four of us—yes, I'm afraid The Bear has to come along; she has become fat and sassy, but she cannot be trusted with the chickens and has to be kept on a chain, silly cow! The four of us repair to the river and rummage for fish bones, sniff at the fox tracks, listen to the geese as the golden sun breaks through the mists, or shudder at the wolf howls ringing clear across the valley and the bear paw prints on the frozen river bars.

And there is always something entertaining going on at Schoolhouse Creek. Like the time we had a party for the old gentleman's 90th birthday (that would have made him 13 years old by dog reckoning, which is no great age—I have already beaten him by a year), and 200 people and four dogs arrived to celebrate. A band had been hired to play in the old schoolroom just along the road, and there was dancing until dawn—and the food! The food!

I also learned many new things of great interest. I have finally come to understand where eggs come from. Until now I had assumed that they were manufactured in their packages like offal in a can. I had never actually associated them with chickens before, as whenever I saw these birds they were behind bars, and I assumed their only purpose was to be eaten. But at Schoolhouse Creek, they are let loose every day to run about the yard, where they flutter their feathers in the dust in the sunshine or troop, wet-feathered and bedraggled, onto the porch of one of the cabins in the rain. And believe it or not, eggs issue directly from chickens' . . . I shall use the word "derrières" for want of a better. When they produce one, the affected creatures announce their achievement with a series of ear-grating cackles that Chris, even in her most furious screech of rage, never comes close to emulating. But the hens' tirades are not delivered in anger; they are merely some kind of misplaced exuberance. Relief at having got a load off their mind, as it were? As soon as I heard it, off I would trot, nose to the ground, and sure enough, in one of their favourite hollows would be at least one, sometimes more, of these offerings. And I didn't need a can opener to open them.

Hens, I was to discover, had other uses apart from the production of food.

The Schoolhouse Creek farm had been, in years gone by, a little fishing resort. Consequently, the yard was occupied by a neat row of cabins, and as the main house was very small, most visitors stayed in these. The cabins had no plumbing; they were served by an outhouse a little way up the hill behind them. The outhouse happened to be situated next to the chicken house, and it therefore made a convenient place to store the chickens' food. The hens liked nothing better than to dive inside the outhouse and peck up spilled grains from the floor; if the door was inadvertently left open, they would return there to roost.

One day, Chris left the outhouse door open, with the consequence that several birds roosted inside. A visitor, upon going up to the building late at night, was startled out of her wits by a cacophonous explosion of hysterics and feathers. The story was laughed about in the morning, and everyone resolved to keep the outhouse door shut in future.

Some weeks later, another visitor went to use the facilities. "Tina," she said, with a puzzled look on her face, "there's a chicken in the outhouse."

The hens liked nothing better than to dive inside the outhouse and roost.

"Oh, they're always getting in there," Chris replied, unconcerned. (She happened to be visiting on that occasion, too.) "They do that every time someone leaves the door open."

"No," said the visitor. "I don't mean just in the outhouse; I mean down the hole."

We stared at her.

Down the hole?

We ran to the little building. Sure enough, in the depths of the dark dungeon, not one, but two hens were quietly walking about.

"My God!" said Tina faintly.

"They must have been knocked down by the other visitors that time I left the door open," said Chris.

"Which means," said Tina, "that they've been down that hole for a month."

There was no way to get them out through the top of the outhouse, so a board was pried off the back. Another board was propped slant-wise into the hole, and after a few minutes, the unfortunate birds walked up it, blinking a little in the unaccustomed daylight.

We stared at them in awe.

What had they lived on all this time?

We looked down into the hole.

It was absolutely clean to the bare, sandy earth.

There wasn't even a scrap of toilet paper left.

We looked again at the hens. They seemed plump and healthy, if a little spaced out, after their ordeal.

"Grab them," said Tina. "We'll have to keep them confined for a while so we don't mix them up with the others."

Then followed a brief flurry as the hens were caught, and by the end of it, the humans were laughing.

"We should hire them out," guffawed Chris, the tears running down her face. "Special environmentally friendly septic-tank cleaning team. We'd make a fortune!"

The two hens, I am pleased to say, laid like troopers.

And you'll never believe this, but we dogs got all their eggs.

*I have become old, and I am content to do little
else but dream away my days and hours.*

CHAPTER TWENTY-THREE

I HAVE BEEN AT SCHOOLHOUSE Creek for a long time now, so long it is sometimes hard to remember that I ever had another life. I have become old. My legs are very stiff, and my hearing has completely gone, although I have learned to lip-read fairly well and rarely miss out on the important things in life. And in truth, as long as I get a few treats and affectionate pats once in a while, I am content to do little else but dream away my days and hours. I think at times of Sport and Chris and Nuk Tessli, but for some reason, the pictures of the cabin at Lonesome Lake and the little shack we had near Salmon Arm, and even the hole I shared with my brothers and sisters along the Atnarko River, seem less confusing than the images of my later exploits and adventures. As I slide into sleep, it is the old man's hands that hold me, and as I run in my dreams and am young again, it is Snoopy who tears along beside me, and the squeakers who sing of my youth.

And I can dream in comfort. For here at Schoolhouse Creek, I at last have what I have always wanted—my own secure bed at night. I have four solid walls to keep out the wild animals, and a woodstove of my very own to keep me warm. I mentioned before that the property was composed of several small cabins, and Tina has appropriated one of these for her studio. It is a very tiny place, barely big enough to swing a cat, but at times three humans and three dogs work in there—and you can imagine how much room that great lummox Oscar takes up.

But at night the place is my own. It is because of the modelling earth, I believe, which must not freeze, that the stove is kept on at night. So it makes an ideal kennel for my old bones.

Old age has been kind to me, for I have generally been in fairly good health. But I have to confess to one of the painfully embarrassing afflictions of old age, that of incontinence. Tina and her apprentices are all late risers, and latterly, to my great shame, I have not always been able to last the night. Tina and her crew are always very kind about it, but when one's body fails to function within one's control, it is always very distressing.

I think Chris arrived yesterday. I'm convinced I saw her and felt her hands, but I am no longer sure anymore what is real and what I have dreamt. Perhaps this is her now; the building trembles with feet climbing the three wooden steps. It is early yet, too early for Tina, for the wintry morning light has not long been seeping through the window.

No, it is not Chris. It is Hans. Perhaps I dreamed Chris after all. I feel Hans's hand upon my head. I lift my eyes to his face, and although his features are indistinct, he seems to be talking to me. His hands are very kind. Is he asking me to go for a walk? He smells of gun oil and newly turned earth, which is odd, for I thought it was winter; it surely can't be time to dig the garden. But perhaps I am mistaken. Maybe it is springtime after all. Perhaps there are squeakers to chase—but was that here or some other place?

And is that the rifle that Hans carries on his back? Doesn't he remember how much I hate that gun? Tina must have forgotten to cut my bangs recently, for I can't make it out very clearly. I don't really want to go for a walk, but Hans is urging me again, even lifting my poor old hips to help me get to my feet. They don't seem to be functioning properly, and in truth I don't feel all that well this morning. I'd much rather just stay here in the warm. But Hans is insisting and guiding me gently to the door. Obedience is the code by which I have always lived, and when I am called, it is my duty to follow. Did Chris say she would be out there? I forget. Did she come yesterday after all? I don't really know anymore. Ah well, if I don't see her, it doesn't really matter. In my mind she will be with me.

And she'll walk along beside me as I go.

PUBLISHER'S NOTE

AT THE END of June 2004, lightning started a fire close to Hunlen Falls. For a month it burned slowly, but on July 24 it exploded. In two days, it roared along the Atnarko River to the west end of Charlotte Lake. All of the homesteaders' buildings near the south end of Lonesome Lake were destroyed, including John Edwards's place and Chris and Lonesome's first cabin. As a 400-person crew battled it, the fire continued to creep along Whitton Creek in the east and as far as the southern tip of Rainbow Lake in the west. The fire was finally put out by heavy rains in late August, and Nuk Tessli was saved.

CHRIS CZAJKOWSKI has lived off the grid in the British Columbia wilderness for the last three decades. Her experiences are recorded in her previous books, *Cabin at Singing River, Diary of a Wilderness Dweller, Nuk Tessli: The Life of a Wilderness Dweller,* and *Snowshoes and Spotted Dick: Letters from a Wilderness Dweller.* Her new book, *And the River Still Sings,* is out this fall with Caitlin Press. She blogs at WildernessDweller.ca.

CHRISTINA CLARKE studied art for five years, four at the Alberta College of Art in Calgary, and one at Dudley College in England. A glassmaker for 25 years, she also paints portraits of both people and animals; her work is featured in a number of animal portrait collections. She has also worked as a scenic artist and painter for numerous movies.